The instant *New York Times* and *USA Today* bestselling book, and one of former President Barack Obama's favorite books of 2017!

When future NBA legend Kareem Abdul-Jabbar was an eighteen-year-old high school basketball prospect from New York City named Lew Alcindor, he accepted a scholarship from UCLA largely on the strength of Coach John Wooden's reputation as a winner.

It turned out to be the right choice, as Alcindor and his teammates won an unprecedented three NCAA championship titles. It also marked the beginning of one of the most extraordinary and enduring friendships in the history of sports.

COACH WOODEN AND ME is a stirring tribute to the subtle but profound influence that Wooden had on Kareem as a player and then as a person. Abdul-Jabbar fondly recalls how Coach Wooden's fatherly guidance paved the way for not only his unmatched professional success but also a lifetime of personal fulfillment.

COACH WOODEN AND ME is at once a celebration of the unique philosophical outlook of college basketball's most storied coach and a moving testament to the all-conquering power of friendship.

Praise for

COACH WOODEN and ME

"This latest masterpiece by Kareem Abdul-Jabbar is even better than all the rest...I'm captivated, enthralled, educated, and entertained as The King's words roll off the page even smoother than his skyhook did off his fingertips."

—Bill Walton

"I always knew my Daddy felt this way about Kareem, but I never knew Kareem ever felt this way about my Dad."

—Nan Wooden, Coach Wooden's Daughter

"An inspirational story."

—ESPN

"Abdul-Jabbar gives a glimpse into his personal growth and evolution...that's what makes COACH WOODEN AND ME such an interesting read. Abdul-Jabbar's book isn't just about a player who butts heads with his coach and later realizes that the coach was trying to help him become a better man type tale. It's a story about two individuals who learned a lot about life from each other."

—*Rolling Stone*

"A miraculous evocation of the ultimate odd couple relationship in sports history."

—*Huffington Post*

"Tender, melancholy, and made me tear up."

—*Los Angeles Review of Books*

"COACH WOODEN AND ME is an inspiring story of friendship between two basketball icons. It is not only an intimate story of their friendship but also the history of basketball. Abdul-Jabbar proves to be as good a storyteller as he was a sportsman. He shines a light on unexplored aspects of their lives. It will inspire not only the fans of Coach John Wooden and Abdul-Jabbar but also basketball lovers."

—*The Washington Book Review*

"Abdul-Jabbar and Wooden shared a priceless friendship, and this sensitive, sharply written account brings it to full, vivid life." —*Booklist* (starred review)

"A pleasant expression of deep appreciation for a man who changed the author's life by enriching it."

—*Kirkus*

"Anyone inclined to dismiss John Wooden and Abdul-Jabbar's relationship as merely coach and player...will rethink that miscalculation after reading this compact, engaging memoir." —*Publisher's Weekly*

"This stunning eulogy will appeal to readers far beyond the confines of sports. Highly recommended."

—*Library Journal*

COACH WOODEN
and ME

Our 50-Year Friendship
On and Off the Court

———

KAREEM ABDUL-JABBAR

GRAND CENTRAL
PUBLISHING

NEW YORK   BOSTON

Grand Central Publishing
Hachette Book Group
1290 Avenue of the Americas, New York, NY 10104
grandcentralpublishing.com
twitter.com/grandcentralpub

First published in hardcover in May 2017.
First Trade Paperback Edition: May 2018.

Grand Central Publishing is a division of Hachette Book Group, Inc.
The Grand Central Publishing name and logo is a trademark of Hachette Book Group, Inc.

The publisher is not responsible for websites (or their content) that are not owned by the publisher.

The Hachette Speakers Bureau provides a wide range of authors for speaking events. To find out more, go to www.hachettespeakersbureau.com or call (866) 376-6591.

Library of Congress Cataloging-in-Publication Data has been applied for.

ISBNs: 978-1-4555-4226-0 (trade paperback), 978-1-4555-4225-3 (ebook)

Printed in the United States of America

LSC-C

10 9 8 7 6 5 4 3 2 1

*To Coach Wooden's family
from somebody who humbly appreciates the fact that
I was allowed to become part of your family.*

Contents

Prologue:
Why It Took Fifty Years to Write This Book   1

1. When Worlds Collide:
Midwestern Hick Meets Harlem Hoopster   11

2. The Game Is Afoot:
It's Never about Winning and Other Courtside Lessons   63

3. Color Blind:
The Unbearable Darkness of Being Black   113

4. What Would Wooden Do:
Religion, Politics, and Keeping the Faith   153

5. We've Got Trouble, Right Here in Pauley Pavilion:
Getting Lost on Wooden Way   187

6. "Time Can Bend Your Knees":
The Hours of Friendship in the Days of Grief   225

7. Our Long Day's Journey into Night   251

Acknowledgments   281

Why It Took Fifty Years to Write This Book

In 2016, I stood in the East Wing of the White House beside twenty of the most famous and accomplished people in the world, all of whom I greatly admired. Among them were Tom Hanks, Robert Redford, Diana Ross, Michael Jordan, Ellen DeGeneres, Bill and Melinda Gates, Bruce Springsteen, Cicely Tyson, and Robert De Niro.

And one other guy.

The president of the United States, Barack Obama.

President Obama bestowed the Presidential Medal of Freedom on each of us, though when he came to me, I had to stoop down so he could reach my neck. He gave brief, complimentary speeches about each of our contributions to America. When President Obama spoke of me, his lavish praise made me squirm a little.

Awards ceremonies always make me uncomfortable. While I appreciate being acknowledged for 1) having done something relevant and 2) still being alive, there's an element of self-aggrandizement that is attached to the ceremony that embarrasses me. I am by nature very shy and don't enjoy talking about myself. I'm that guy at the party sitting behind the potted palm—as long as it's a really big potted palm. What I appreciated most about what President Obama said was that I wasn't up there just because of my basketball career, but also because of my seventeen years of writing books and articles about social injustice toward people of color, women, the LGBT community, Muslims, and immigrants ("he is advocating on Capitol Hill or writing with extraordinary eloquence about patriotism"). Then another thought hip-checked in: If there wasn't social injustice, would I even be getting this medal? Was I somehow benefiting from social injustice? What kind of monster does that?!

Who has such thoughts while receiving the country's highest civilian award? Why couldn't I just be grateful, smile, and think, "Presidential Medal of Freedom. Cool."

President Obama closed the ceremony by saying, "Everyone on this stage has touched me in a powerful personal way. These are folks who have helped make me who I am." That's when I knew exactly why I felt so uncomfortable.

Someone was missing.

The man who, more than anyone else in my life, was responsible for me standing in the exact same spot where he had stood thirteen years earlier. That's when President George W. Bush awarded Coach John Wooden the same Presidential Medal of Freedom I had just received. I could still remember what President Bush had said about Coach's relationship with his students: "Coach Wooden remains a part of their lives as a teacher of the game, and as an example of what a good man should be."

I looked out at the audience applauding us and wished Coach were among them. His guiding hand at UCLA had only been the start. After that, we developed a friendship that grew closer and closer over the next four decades. We celebrated our triumphs together and helped each other through dark tragedies together. As I grew up, played professional basketball, married, had children, lost loved ones, retired, and changed careers, I never grew away from Coach's influence. Even on that day, the medal hanging heavily around my neck, I knew what he would have said: "Kareem, don't overthink it. Enjoy the moment. Don't let yesterday take up too much of today."

I looked down the line of the wonderfully successful people on either side of me and wondered if each of them had a Coach Wooden who, to quote President Obama, "helped make me who I am." I hoped so, because without Coach, my life would have been so much less. Less joyous. Less meaningful. Less filled with love.

Later, at the reception for the recipients, my business manager Deborah Morales asked me how it felt to receive such a prestigious honor.

"Cool," I said, remembering my earlier admonishment to relax.

She laughed. "Some writer, if that's all you can come up with."

I thought for a moment, looking for something pretentiously writerly. "'With mirth and laughter let old wrinkles come.' I'm feeling mirthy."

Deborah touched my arm. "You're thinking of him, aren't you? Of Coach."

I raised my eyebrows in surprise. "How did you know?"

"How could you not be? He helped make this happen." She gestured around the room full of famous people to indicate "this." "Plus, you're quoting something literary, just like he always did. Whenever you do that, you're thinking of him."

* * *

John Wooden died in 2010. So why did I wait seven years to write this book?

Because of something he taught me over the nearly fifty years of our friendship. When I played for Coach Wooden at UCLA, he was very hands-on. He would follow us up and down the sideline barking encouragement and instructions. Then he would pull an individual aside to demonstrate a shot, a pick, a fake. His face always seemed inches from ours. But sometimes he would go all the way to the top rafters of Pauley Pavilion, where all he had to do was raise his arm to touch the ceiling. From there he would look down on us like a benevolent god, watching us scuttle up and down the court. He liked the fresh perspective that gave him. A way to see the big picture. Watch how all the moving parts worked together.

That's what I had to do with our many years of friendship. I had to climb over the seven years since his death to view what it all meant, measure how great his impact on me and others was. This book is that view. I could have written a book about him after I left UCLA. Or after I retired from the pros. Or after Coach died. But those books wouldn't have been *this* book. This book spans almost fifty years of an evolving friendship seen through the eyes of a man who is old enough and mature enough to understand the truth about our relationship, even when I was too young at the time to recognize those truths myself.

Coach Wooden's most important lesson was that we should never focus on the outcome but on the activity itself. "Don't think about winning the game," he'd say. "Just do everything possible to prepare. As long as you know you have done everything possible and you have given your best self on the court, that is your reward.

The scoreboard is meaningless." This philosophy, which became the basis for his time as an English teacher and coach, was inspired by an anonymously written poem he read in college:

> Before God's footstool to confess
> A poor soul knelt and bowed his head
> "I failed," he wailed. The Master said,
> "Thou did thy best, that is success."

Trying to apply his philosophy solely toward winning would be like doing good deeds only because you hope it will get you into heaven. Being good *is* the payoff, athletically and spiritually. That's why he didn't care for sports movies in which the underdog team or player learns the hard way that winning isn't everything, but then they go on to win at the end. To him, those movies should have ended with the lesson learned, the team taking the court happy in their newfound wisdom, the whistle blowing to start the game, and then freeze-frame and run credits. Showing the team winning sends the wrong message: that life lessons exist to serve as a guide for acquiring things that make you feel like a success. His point was that the life lesson *is* the success. The traveling is the reward, not reaching the destination.

This book is not just an appreciation of our friendship or an acknowledgment of Coach Wooden's deep influence on my life. It is the realization that some lives are so extraordinary and touch so many people that their story must be told to generations to come so those values aren't diminished or lost altogether.

Coach was an old white Midwesterner with old-fashioned ideals; I was a quiet but cocky black kid from New York City who towered eighteen inches over him. He was a devout Christian; I became a devout Muslim. He loved big band music of the swing era; I loved modern jazz. On paper, it's understandable that we would have a good working relationship as coach and player. But nothing on that same paper would even hint that we would have a close friendship that would endure a lifetime.

Coach's favorite novel was *The Robe* by Lloyd C. Douglas about the crucifixion of Jesus. He reread it many times and quoted freely from it. One passage from the book he particularly liked was this:

> Our life is like a land journey, too even and easy and dull over long distances across the plains, too hard and painful up the steep grades; but, on the summits of the mountain, you have a magnificent view—and feel exalted—and your eyes are full of happy tears—and you want to sing—and wish you had wings! And then—you can't stay there, but must continue your journey— you begin climbing down the other side, so busy

with your footholds that your summit experience
is forgotten.

Over the course of our friendship, Coach and I
climbed that mountain to share the magnificent view.
This book is my attempt to make sure that our summit
experience is not forgotten and that others can make
that same climb and be filled with happy tears.

Chapter 1

When Worlds Collide

Midwestern Hick Meets
Harlem Hoopster

"A coach's primary function should be not to make better players, but to make better people."
—*John Wooden*

A few years ago I was in Chantilly, Virginia, sitting behind a table signing sports memorabilia. Autographing sessions are tricky because whenever I look up I see hundreds of people who have been standing patiently for an hour or more for just ten seconds of time with me. Some want to tell long stories about how watching me play was a bonding experience with their father. Or that they were at the Boston game in 1971 when I scored fifty points. Some just want to quote *Airplane!*: "My name is Roger Murdock. I'm the copilot." I always laugh because they get such a kick out of it. I try to engage as much as possible and still keep the line moving. I'd see an elderly man at the back of the line wearing an ancient UCLA jersey, worry about how long he'd hold up, and start signing faster.

I had been signing for about a half hour when a man in a Lakers cap laid down a composite photograph in front of me. "You seen this?" he asked.

I picked it up and studied it. It only took a second before I felt my heart cinch a little.

This composite consisted of two photographs, side by side, of me with John Wooden, my former coach at UCLA, who had died two years earlier. I had seen both photographs, but I had never seen them put together in this way. I was so startled that I forgot about keeping the line moving or the old man in the UCLA jersey. The photo on the left was a posed black-and-white picture taken at center court in the then brand-new Pauley Pavilion in 1966. Coach Wooden is robust and ruddy-cheeked, dressed in a dark suit and tie, looking like the traveling preacher he might well have become in another life. I'm wearing a practice uniform and staring at him devotedly as he pretends to demonstrate some move to me. I knew the photo had been taken in 1966 during my sophomore season because of my stylish two-inch Afro that dipped low over my forehead. I couldn't have even guessed the decade from Coach Wooden's styling. As always, his gray hair was neatly parted on the left side in a line so straight he might have used a ruler with the comb. It obviously was a posed media photo because, as formal as he was, he never wore a tie to practice. Practice was for working hard, and wearing a tie was for game time or sitting behind a desk.

The candid color photo on the right was also taken at Pauley Pavilion, although by this time the court had been named after Coach and his wife, Nellie. It was shot after a game in 2007, forty years after the first one. In this photo, the two of us are walking off the court hand-in-hand. He is wearing another dark suit, which seemed a little too big for him, but instead of a regular tie, he wore a bolo tie with a large turquoise stone at the throat. He'd taken to wearing those in his last few years because of his love for Western films, which he and I had spent many pleasurable hours watching together. I was wearing jeans, a leather jacket, and a belt with a big silver buckle that looked like a holster should dangle from it. We were an odd pair of desperados.

I raised the photo closer to my face, willing myself back to that moment. That special moment I had never forgotten.

He looked very frail, slightly bent, leaning on a cane, but even in that photograph there is a determination in his posture—and, as usual, every strand of hair is perfectly in place. I let myself drift back to that moment, even as I felt a deep melancholy tighten my throat.

I had been walking quickly after the game, my head bowed, actively oblivious to everything around, like a guy in a prison break, so I wouldn't get stopped. Once that happens, inevitably, a crowd gathers. I always feel like an ungrateful jerk when I'm doing that power walk through crowds, but if I slow down, programs, hats, and jerseys are thrust in my face, and it's at least an hour before I get back to my car and two before I'm home. Sometimes I just want to go home.

But suddenly I heard his familiar voice, and it stopped me dead in my escape. "Hey, Kareem."

I turned with a big grin on my face. "Coach," I said, "How's it going?" I leaned forward to embrace him, but as I did, he took my hand in his and gripped it tightly. His small hand in mine felt like a child's.

"It's going good," he said. Then he added, almost apologetically, "Kareem, would you give me a hand, please?"

He wasn't holding my hand just for affection, he needed me to help him walk. And he trusted me not to make a big deal of it.

"Sure, Coach," I said, as if we'd done this a hundred times before.

We walked off the court together. Fans shouted, "Hey, Coach!" or "Yo, Kareem!" but no one approached us. They could see that it would not be prudent to stop Coach's slow but steady progress. True fans have a sixth sense about these things.

I walked slowly with him through the players' tunnel where his daughter, Nan, was waiting for him. I hugged her, then hugged Coach, a bit more gingerly, and said goodbye.

It was to be our last time together on a basketball court. On the drive home I thought I'd be sad and have to crank up some Miles Davis to get me through the emotion. But I wasn't sad. I felt joy that I was able to be there for Coach the way he had been there for me so often. Walking him across the court, I had felt tenderness, protectiveness, but not pity or sorrow. I was smiling.

I ran my long finger over the photo as if I could touch him one last time. Lend him the strength I tried to give him that night. I'm not one for easy sentiment, but Coach could always bring it out in me, even now. Looking at him in his black suit and with his cane, I was reminded of Charlie Chaplin's irrepressible Tramp, strolling happily through life no matter the hardships and obstacles. And here we were strolling through it together, just as we had for almost fifty years.

I sat there at that table in Chantilly, Virginia, staring at those photographs, the bookends of one of the most meaningful relationships of my life. I cleared my throat before speaking. "No, I hadn't seen this," I said to the man who had put it in front of me. I smiled up at him. "But thank you."

I signed it for him and he moved along, unaware of the effect his ten seconds had had on me. The next person stepped in front of the table and I signed a photo, and then another and yet another. And so it went until the elderly man in the old UCLA jersey shook my hand and said, "You think the Lakers are gonna pull it out this year?" I lingered a little on the handshake, remembering Coach's hand, light and fragile as a hummingbird, and said, "I hope so."

It's appropriate that the first photo is black-and-white. That accurately defined our rigid relationship in the beginning. In this photo he is leading me. He was the coach; I was his player. He made the rules; I followed them. Black and white. Mutual respect but not warmth. It's also appropriate that we were posed, because we both look a little awkward, stiff as mannequins in a store window. As if there were something artificial about the roles we were forced to play in the photo and in life.

The second photo, with its rich, warm colors and candid appearance, more accurately reflected the depth of our friendship. Our two hands—one fragile and one strong, one white and one black—entwined. His white head barely clears my elbow, yet I am standing straight and proud, like a man showing off his hero dad. In that photo, I appear to be leading him. But knowing how much he taught me, I knew I was still following in his footsteps, even though he was beside me.

* * *

John Wooden has been honored as the greatest coach in American sports history. He was dubbed "The Wizard of Westwood" (which he hated) due to his unprecedented knack for winning. Before he retired in 1975, he had brought UCLA a total of ten national championships, seven of them consecutively, at one point leading the school to an eighty-eight-game winning streak. That earned him his own place in the Basketball Hall of Fame. He was very proud of that, although I never heard him mention that he was the first person ever to be inducted into the Basketball Hall of Fame as both a player and, later, as a coach. The philosophy he crafted for living a full and satisfying life, the Pyramid of Success, has become a widely popular motivational tool that has been taught to thousands nationwide. His coaching methods have been adopted by high schools, colleges, and universities around the world. Even major businesses have used his teachings to build better teamwork among employees. His influence far surpassed the ninety-four-by-fifty-foot dimensions of the basketball court where he lived most of his life.

But for me, he was much more than a basketball guru. He was also my teacher, my friend, and, though I never told him, my role model.

We won three national championships together. I was an All-American each of those years. I set records— not as many as I would have set under another coach, but as many as the team needed set in order to win. I took the game I had learned from him into professional basketball, where eventually I played my way into the Hall of Fame, right beside him.

Our relationship had been born over basketball, but eventually that became the least important aspect of it. Our friendship blossomed and grew over shared values, over complicated loves and devastating losses, over a never truly satisfied search for understanding of this world and our place in it. In later years, I would sit with him at his home, quietly watching a Western movie or baseball game on his small TV, just enjoying the familiar warmth and comfort of his presence. The afternoon would pass in his cozy den, and I would feel ready to face the world outside again. It was like going to church.

* * *

I first met John Wooden on a recruiting trip to UCLA in March of 1965. When I saw that his office was in a squat World War II Quonset hut, the bright Los Angeles sun glinting off the shiny corrugated steel, I worried that the campus couldn't afford proper offices for its coaches and was forced to shove them in army huts. At the same time, I thought it looked kind of cool, like a science fiction film: astronauts' living quarters on Mars protecting them from giant mutant Martian spiders. My many hours of reading and watching TV had left me with the knack of romanticizing any situation.

The hut was among several that sat like eggs in a nest adjacent to Westwood Boulevard. On the walk to the huts, I saw various exotic flowers I'd never seen before, all in full spring bloom. "Those are she-oaks," my enthusiastic campus guide said, as she pointed at some plants. "And that's weeping wattle, over there are bristly oxtongue. Those are sausage trees. Indigenous to Africa." She smiled as if the connection to Africa would tip me into choosing UCLA. African sausage trees? Really?

Still, this was more green than I'd ever seen outside of Central Park. I already knew I wanted to come here. The previous summer I'd accidentally gotten caught up in a violent riot in Harlem. Gunshots had popped all around me. Angry protesters had spilled over from a gathering outside the police station where they were demanding answers concerning the shooting death of a fifteen-year-old black boy, James Powell, by Lieutenant Thomas Gilligan. They had set fires and smashed store windows. Looters had pushed their way through the crowds to grab what they could. I'd run with the other fleeing Harlemites, trying to keep my head low to make myself a smaller target. Even crouching, I still hovered over everyone else. I had never been so scared in my life as that night. But I'd also never been so angry at the police, who dismissed the protesters by shouting, "Go home!" Holding up photos of the young victim, protesters hollered back, "We are home!"

The nation was still in racial turmoil. Malcolm X had just been assassinated the month before my visit to UCLA. A few weeks before my visit, civil rights leader John Lewis had led six hundred marchers across the Edmund Pettus Bridge in Selma, Alabama, only to be met by police who shot tear gas at them and beat them with billy clubs, hospitalizing fifty of the protestors. Quickly dubbed "Bloody Sunday," the march had been televised around the world. Two weeks later, Dr. Martin Luther King, Jr., led another group of protestors across the bridge, this time under federal protection. They successfully crossed.

I had been wrestling with my role in all of this. I wanted to do my part for civil rights, but at almost eighteen, I needed some time to think about what my part would be. California seemed like the perfect place to figure that out.

"Welcome, Lewis," John Wooden said as I entered his office. He wore a pressed white shirt almost as bright as the California sun outside and a black tie. His sport jacket hung on the hat rack in the corner. His short hair was parted almost down the middle, reminding me of Alfalfa, the squeaky-voiced kid in the Little Rascal movies I used to watch on TV. His voice had a nasally Midwestern lilt that I found amusing after the harsh New York accents I was used to.

Over the years, people have asked me if I was nervous that day meeting the great John Wooden. I probably should have been, but I wasn't. Instead, I was anxious and impatient, ready to get my college life going. Ready to start playing serious basketball. I didn't doubt my ability to do well playing with college-level players, and I was ready to prove it to him and anybody else. I might have borrowed my attitude from Marlon Brando as the motorcycle rebel in *The Wild One*. "What are you rebelling against, Johnny?" To which Marlon as Johnny says, "Whadda ya got?"

"I'm impressed with your grades, Lewis," he said as we sat across from each other, his crowded desk between us.

Grades? I thought. You're the coach of one of the best basketball teams in the country and you're talking grades? What about my impressive stats?

He looked me straight in the eyes to make sure I knew he was serious. "For most students, basketball is temporary. But knowledge is forever."

I nodded agreement. "Yes, sir." I hadn't expected academics to be the first thing we'd talk about, but I came to learn that academics, not basketball, were the first priority on Coach Wooden's agenda for his players. His players would graduate with grades that would give them career opportunities beyond sports. He was worried about our long-term happiness, not our win–loss record. I had visited other universities and talked to lots of coaches who touted their schools' sports programs, comely coeds, and national reputation, but Coach Wooden was the first to make a point of talking about grades and classes. He didn't treat me as a basketball player, but as a student who would be playing basketball on the side.

We talked for about thirty minutes, only briefly touching on basketball. He told me that most often he recruited players for quickness rather than size, and he had never coached someone as tall as I was, but he added, "I'm sure we will find the proper way to use you on the court. I am looking forward to coaching someone like you."

We stood and shook hands again.

"Freshman year can be very difficult," he warned. "Making that transition from high school isn't easy. There are a lot of adjustments, especially for athletes, who have to train every day for several hours."

I nodded again.

He smiled. "But you seem like the kind of young man up to the challenge."

The challenge. That's what I was looking for in a school, and somehow he knew that. Rather than tell me how easily I would fit in and how smoothly everything would go, he appealed to the competitor in me. And, to quote one of his favorite Robert Frost poems, "That has made all the difference."

* * *

As I learned later, our first meeting was perfectly representative of his philosophy of recruiting: "I wanted young men who wanted to play for UCLA, and not one that I had to talk into playing for UCLA. I always believed that the way to build a great team is to find the kind of people you want to work with and tell them the truth."

He certainly told the truth. In fact, he may be the only coach in college basketball history who recruited a talented player by telling him he would rarely play. Playing for Coach Wooden made you a member of his team forever. Through the years, through reunions and at events, eventually you got to meet and often become friends with people who had played for him at different times. It was like joining an exclusive club. Among the former players I've met and have become friends with is Swen Nater.

Swen Nater was a six-foot-eleven-inch Community College All-American in 1970, averaging twenty-six points and fourteen rebounds. Nater had been transformed from a big clumsy kid to a talented player by Don Johnson, his coach at Cypress College, who years earlier had been Coach Wooden's very first All-American at UCLA. Nater had become a very desirable transfer student and was being strongly recruited by several major programs. But Johnson had filled Nater's head with tales of John Wooden and UCLA basketball, then talked Wooden into offering him a scholarship. Wooden actually tried to talk him out of accepting it, telling him, "Swen, if you come to UCLA, you're probably not going to play much because we've got this big redheaded kid from San Diego named Bill Walton coming in, and he's quite a talent." Then he added, "But you'll have the opportunity to play against the best center in the nation in practice every day. And I believe that is going to give you a better chance of becoming a professional basketball player than if you were to go to another school."

Everything Wooden said came true. Nater didn't play very much at UCLA, but eventually became the first player never to start a college game to be drafted in the first round by the National Basketball Association (NBA). And as Coach Wooden had predicted, he eventually played twelve seasons of professional basketball, even leading the NBA in rebounding one year.

Coach Wooden recruited character as much as ability. He wanted a certain kind of person, so he studied the background of potential recruits, explaining, "I could learn so much about each individual by studying the environment that he had been around before I would have him come to UCLA." To find out as much as possible, on occasion he would make home visits. He told me once that during one of those visits—although, as typically, he never mentioned this person's name—a potential recruit snapped at his mother for a comment she made, and at that moment lost his chance to play for John Wooden. He explained, "I did not want a person who was that disrespectful on my team."

As impressive as Coach Wooden was, I was equally persuaded to go to UCLA when assistant coach Jerry Norman showed me the new arena that would be Pauley Pavilion, then under construction. "The first event at the new arena will be the annual varsity-freshmen game," he said as casually as he could. I knew what he meant: if I came to UCLA, I'd be playing in that game.

* * *

The next time we met was in May at my home in Manhattan. We lived on the fifth floor in a tiny two-bedroom apartment on Nagle Avenue in the Dyckman Houses project. With all the offers I had received, Coach Wooden was the only coach my parents invited to our apartment.

Coach Wooden arrived with Jerry Norman, both wearing sport coats and ties. I introduced them to my parents, and the four of them sat in the living room to discuss my future. I had already decided to attend UCLA, so this meeting was a formality to make my parents feel good about me moving three thousand miles away from their domineering presence into the care of total strangers.

I seemed to be the only person in the room who was nervous. I needed this to go well.

My dad was a cop, and he faced them with his cop's poise. My mom was devoted to protecting her only child, and she would face down armies to do so. Tough audience.

"Lewis," my mom said, "why don't you go wait in your room while we talk."

Sure, Mom, I thought with some annoyance. I'll wait in my room like a Jane Austen heroine while the grown-ups discuss my future. But I went without a word. In a few months I'd be out of the house and living free in glorious California.

For the next hour I strained to listen through the walls to what they were saying. Unsuccessfully. When I was finally called back into the living room, we shook hands and said our goodbyes.

Whatever Coach Wooden had said impressed my parents. "He's very dignified," my father said.

"A gentleman," my mom said. "Not the kind of man who'd take advantage of you." She was worried that a school might try to exploit me. We'd heard stories about college athletes who got injured and lost their scholarships. Coach Wooden had assured them he would look out for me, and they believed him.

My parents weren't pushovers. I remember how amazed I was that Coach Wooden, through his quiet integrity, was so easily able to assuage my parents' fears for their child. The more I got to know him, the more

I would try to emulate his understated poise, which would sometimes be mistaken for aloofness.

Years later we were sitting in his den, and I asked him if he even remembered that visit. "Well, of course I do," he said.

"Really?" I found it hard to believe.

"Oh, yes. I remember being quite impressed by your apartment."

"Now I know you don't remember. That apartment was small and cramped."

"Not how I remember it," he said. "Everything was neat and clean and well organized. The carefully framed family photos on the walls showed a loving family and a stable environment. Care had been taken." He smiled. "It was all pluses."

My parents must have made an impression on him, too. When I announced my decision to attend UCLA at a press conference about a week after his visit, Coach Wooden told the media, "This boy is not only a fine student and a great college basketball prospect, but he is also a refreshingly modest young man who shows the results of excellent parental and high school training.

"After meeting Mr. and Mrs. Alcindor, I could easily understand the fine impression Lew made on all of us when he visited our campus. Their guidance has enabled him to handle the fame and adulation that has come his way in a most gracious and unaffected manner."

When my parents heard that, they were ready to adopt him into the family. I admit to feeling proud that he saw me as modest and relieved that he had complimented my parents so publicly when he didn't have to. As far as coaches went, all pluses.

* * *

So far, there was no reason to think that this middle-aged white man with the 1930s haircut would become the greatest influence on my life. I was Lewis Alcindor, an eighteen-year-old seven-foot-two-inch black kid from New York City. I was all about fast subways, hot jazz, and civil rights politics. He was John Wooden, a fifty-five-year-old five-foot-ten-inch white man from a hick town in Indiana. He was all about, what? Tractors, big bands, and Christian morals? We were an odd-couple sitcom waiting to happen.

Our only common denominator was the game of basketball. At first, that was enough.

When we first met, I was a very shy young man. The basketball court was the one place where I was assertive and capable of being aggressive. Beyond that, I was trying to deal with a society changing rapidly around me. I was learning how to be a black man in America at a most difficult time in our national history. I felt guilty that I was living a privileged life playing basketball in California, studying at a top university, while other kids my age were being denied the same opportunities because of the color of their skin. Watching Dr. King's marches, I itched to do something to join the fight. But I didn't want to sacrifice my future. Was I being a hypocrite or helping the cause by getting my education?

My parents, as well as Jack Donahue, my coach at Power Memorial Academy, were hardworking people who expected me to do well, and that required discipline and application on my part. They taught me that it was cool to be smart and gave me the support that I needed. They made it very clear to me that playing basketball was not my goal, it was a means to achieve my dreams. Even after it had become obvious that I had the talent to play basketball professionally, they reminded me how easily I could get hurt and that the only thing I could depend on was a good education.

Here's how serious I was about education: When I was in fourth grade my parents sent me to the Holy Providence School. The other kids did not appreciate the fact that I was a good student, so I was singled out as a nerd. They called me the egghead. Honestly, I sort of liked that—it was nice drawing attention to myself because I was smart rather than because I was tall.

My mother was a seamstress who had grown up in the Jim Crow South in Wadesboro, North Carolina, and had, at most, a junior high school education. We never talked about it, we never talked about the life she had lived in Wadesboro, North Carolina. But she pushed me, she continuously pushed me to be better, to work harder. She was a very pragmatic woman, and she had dreams for me long before I had my own. Education mattered in our home. I remember her pointing out to me that the great boxing champion Joe Louis did not speak very well. He stuttered when he spoke and at times had difficulty expressing himself. "I don't want you to be like him," she told me. "I want you to be like Jackie Robinson." It often was pointed out to me that the Dodgers' great Robinson was a college graduate. My parents were far more proud of the fact that I made the honor roll in grade school and high school than the fact that I scored a lot of points on the court. They gave me ambition and direction.

My father was a New York transit police officer, eventually becoming a lieutenant in the department. But his real passion was music; that was his world. My father was not an especially social person; he lacked the social graces that my mom had in abundance. Instead, he expressed his feelings through his music. He played in local groups in Harlem, although he was never able to make a living at it. He was a fine section player, a team player, but he was not a memorable soloist. He was the type of musician who would have done well in the trombone section of a big band. He never really got the opportunity. I remember him telling me a story about a missed audition. He loved Count Basie, who apparently needed a trombonist for his band. Playing for Count Basie would have been his dream come true. He had been at work, though, and didn't learn about the audition until he got home. He grabbed his trombone and ran down to the audition hall. But by the time he arrived, Count Basie had already hired someone and left.

In some ways my father's musical career was like a sentence ending with a comma: There should have been more to it. He didn't talk about it, but his disappointment was clear. I vowed I was not going to live an unfinished life; I intended to keep trying until I reached the period at the end.

The highlight of his musical career probably was playing in the police department band when it backed up Marilyn Monroe as she sang "Happy Birthday" to President John F. Kennedy at Madison Square Garden in 1962. My father attended Juilliard on the GI Bill, where he focused on the trombone. However, in order for him to pass his piano class, he had to learn how to play the "Moonlight Sonata" on the piano. He practiced, and practiced; day and night all we heard was "Moonlight Sonata," "Moonlight Sonata," "Moonlight Sonata." Eventually, I dabbled with playing a number of instruments, but the one piece I refused to play on any instrument was "Moonlight

Sonata." My problem growing up was that I didn't like reading music, so Mom and Dad agreed to stop my music lessons and instead enrolled me in Little League. While certainly I got my love of jazz from my dad, listening to him practice "Moonlight Sonata" day after day taught me that to be good at something, at anything, you have to work at it and work at it.

Perhaps one reason I eventually fit so well into Coach Wooden's program was that my parents had laid the same strong foundation that Coach often preached to us: "Don't hope. Hope is for people who aren't prepared." My mother always emphasized that hard work was necessary to achieve your goals, while my father proved the value of repetition in mastering a skill.

It was just unfortunate for me that his skill was playing "Moonlight Sonata."

While I didn't get my father's musical talent, I did inherit his ethnic pride. My mother and father had lived different lives. Growing up in the South caused my mother to be soft-spoken about race, she carried the psychological scars of her upbringing, and so she carried secrets with her. I didn't know until I was in my twenties that her mother, my grandmother, had had an affair with a wealthy white landowner and that my mother actually had been married and had two children before meeting my father. The segregated South was swampy with secrets.

My father did not know about any of this any more than I did. I had two half-siblings I knew nothing about until I was twenty-three years old. They would come up to New York and stay with a cousin in Queens. My mother would make up some excuse and visit them. Why she kept this secret I will never know. Despite my repeated questions, she took her reasons to the grave.

My half-brother and half-sister knew about me long before I was aware of their existence. We eventually met and developed our relationships. Both my brother and sister have died, but I have maintained a relationship with my sister's daughter, my niece.

My father took great pride in being a strong black man. His parents were both Garveyites, supporters of the legendary black nationalist leader Marcus Garvey. I remember him talking at great length about their conversations. My father was not a man who ever took a step backward because of his color, and that was the most important lesson I learned from him. I grew up in the middle of the civil rights movement that people like my father had nurtured. Living in New York, in Harlem, for a time I had been somewhat isolated from the reality of race relations in this country. I had both black and white friends and hadn't really been confronted with overt racism. I began to understand more about it in 1962, when my parents put me on a Greyhound bus and sent me to Goldsboro, North

Carolina, to attend the graduation of their best friend's daughter. This was the same time Freedom Riders were taking buses into the Deep South and sitting in at lunch counters. Black Americans were being attacked with high-pressure water hoses, electric cattle prods, and police dogs.

I watched the CBS *Evening News* every night, and Walter Cronkite did a fine job documenting the racial discord, but it had never been so personal until I got on that Greyhound in New York and rode South. When we crossed the Potomac River into Virginia, I saw the signs: white grocery store, white luncheonette, colored rest rooms. I had never so openly experienced the concept of "separate but equal." One look at the fancy white stores and the run-down "colored" stores and I realized that, although they were separate, they certainly weren't equal. I didn't know the rules and even had to ask an older black man, "Am I allowed to walk on the same side of the street as the white people?"

That was my introduction to the cost of being a young black man in the American South.

I became more sensitive to the subtle, but still dangerous, racism in the North. I began to see the walls that always had been there but previously had been invisible to me. One day in religion class at my high school, Power Memorial, a white teacher explained to me that "black people want too much too soon." Too much? We were celebrating the hundredth anniversary of the Emancipation Proclamation. Too soon? I remember my disgust at being forced to say the things this teacher expected to hear if I wanted to get a good grade.

In the summer of 1964 I was hired by the city-funded Harlem Youth Action Project to write for the organization's weekly newspaper. To do that I had to learn about the African-American community, and by doing that I began to learn about myself and my own history. That opened up my world in ways I couldn't have imagined; it changed my life, and it never closed again. My assignments forced me to explore Harlem for the first time in my life. I discovered the Schomburg Center for Research in Black Culture and began to learn about the vibrant artistic history that had come alive in the Harlem Renaissance of the 1920s. I read the work of the great black poets, like Langston Hughes and Countee Cullen. I read Richard Wright's novels and the writings of Marcus Garvey and the black revolutionary W. E. B. DuBois. I began to learn more about the music my father so loved, Count Basie and Louis Armstrong and the birth of jazz on those streets.

And it wasn't just history; when I walked the streets of Harlem the movement was happening all around me. Malcolm X was standing on the corner. Black nationalists were handing out newspapers. People were wearing colorful African clothing. I was a teenager when I covered Dr. Martin Luther King's press conference. And my rite of passage was getting caught up in the summer riots, running for my life as gunfire exploded around me. The world was changing around me, and it was dangerous. Black Americans were standing up for their rights; this country would never be the same again. This fight was to become an essential part of my life.

*   *   *

John Wooden was born into a different world. It was almost as if he had grown up in a painting even Norman Rockwell would call corny. He was born on a farm in rural Hall, Indiana, in 1910. The farm had no running water, no electricity, and his family ate what they grew. In the winter for heat they warmed bricks in the stove and wrapped them in towels. The toilet was an outhouse in the yard. When he spoke to me of those times, he spoke fondly, never with bitterness.

"At night," he told me once, "we read, mostly. There wasn't television, we didn't have radio. Dad would read to us in the evenings. He read the Bible every day and insisted that we did, too. Sometimes, he'd read poetry to us. I can recall him reading Longfellow's 'The Song of Hiawatha.' 'On the shores of Gitche Gumee, Of the shining Big-Sea-Water...' "

It sure wasn't Langston Hughes.

"They called me John-Bob," he said, and I burst out laughing.

"Come on, Coach. You're making this stuff up. John-Bob? Who was your best friend? Billy-Joe? Tommy-Bo?"

He ignored my interruption and continued. He grew up working in the fields and playing baseball and basketball with his three brothers. A ball of rags substituted for a baseball and a bigger ball of rags was his basketball, which he became skilled at tossing into a tomato basket. Although he achieved legendary success in basketball, his first love always was baseball. He knew every baseball statistic. Even more than basketball. Baseball had also been my favorite sport growing up. We argued about our favorite baseball players for five decades without ever really agreeing.

When his father lost the farm in the Depression, the Woodens moved into the little town of Martinsville. There was no racial unrest in that part of southern Indiana; the local chapter of the Ku Klux Klan made certain of that. The Klan was very strong in that area, but he never talked about it. The only thing I ever heard him say about that was, "I had nothing to do with any of that foolishness."

His father also taught him moral lessons, bedrock Midwestern American values. Coach Wooden told a story about that move to Martinsville and the tragedy that followed that summed up his father. His father, Joshua Wooden, had bought some hogs for the family farm in 1925, but to do so he had had to take out a mortgage on their farm. He also bought a batch of vaccine to protect those pigs against cholera. Unfortunately, that vaccine was tainted, and the entire herd died. Later that summer, a drought destroyed the family's crops. Unable to make mortgage payments, Joshua was forced to sell the farm. The family moved into Martinsville where he found work as an attendant at a sanitarium. Although people urged him to take action against the man who had sold him the vaccine, the inference being he might have been able to save the family farm, he wouldn't do it. As Coach Wooden once said of his father, "He refused to speak an unkind word against anyone."

Coach Wooden was exactly the same way. In fifty years I literally can't recall him saying anything unkind about someone else. I could tell when he had a problem with a person because he would avert his eyes and change the subject.

The principles on which John Wooden built his own philosophy, those same principles that would eventually make such a strong impact on me and on so many other people, came from his father. He once said, "I probably didn't appreciate my father at all. But thinking back, some of the things he did became so meaningful. I didn't realize it at the time." Ironically, that is precisely how his players felt about Coach. We weren't aware that we were learning what he was teaching until we needed that knowledge years later.

"My father tried to get across to us never try to be better than someone else." That was among the core beliefs on which his entire philosophy was built. I can't begin to count the number of times I heard him say this. "Learn from others and never cease trying to be the best you can possibly be...If you get yourself too engrossed in things over which you have no control, it's going to adversely affect the things over which you have control."

His dad was especially fond of moral values that came in sets of three. "One was 'Never lie, never cheat, and never steal.' The other one was 'Don't whine, don't complain, and don't alibi.' He tried to get those ideas across not in so many words, but by his actions. The way he walked through life." Years later, Coach Wooden's carefully laid out Pyramid of Success would become a blueprint for leading a productive, rewarding life, but it started with these two sets of threes.

He had begun playing organized basketball in grade school. He was a natural athlete. "I didn't have as much size as many," he said. "But I was quicker than most, and that was my strength." He led his Martinsville high school team to the state championships three times, winning in 1927. Even then, Indiana was basketball crazy. Martinsville had only 4,800 citizens—but the high school gym seated 5,200 and was always filled. Apparently, they would have won their second championship the following year, but in the last few seconds a Muncie Central player heaved a desperation underhand shot from half court that nearly hit the roof before dropping straight through the basket for a 13–12 victory. Coach spent eight decades playing and watching basketball and always said that was the most incredible shot he had ever seen.

Had that story come from anyone else, I might not have believed it. But in all the years of our friendship, I never heard him tell a story that later proved untrue or exaggerated or that in any way glorified him.

However, even my loyalty to his stories was tested one morning when we were having breakfast together at VIP's, a restaurant near his condo where he ordered the same meal "the first seven days of every week." We had just finished debating the pros and cons of the yellow bell-bottom pants some guy at the counter was wearing when out of nowhere he said, "You know, Knute Rockne recruited me to play football at Notre Dame."

"Do I need to check your coffee for rum?" I joked. "You weigh about as much as my left leg."

"It's true."

"Right," I said, expecting this would turn into a joke, and he would laugh at my gullibility. "Did you play football in high school?"

He shook his head. "We didn't even have a football team."

"We talking about the same Notre Dame? Best team in the country at that time?"

"Yup," he insisted. "Knute Rockne himself asked me if I would be interested in coming to Notre Dame to play football for him."

"Knute Rockne? The 'win one for the Gipper' guy?"

He nodded. "He told me he had seen me playing basketball and knew I had the agility, the speed, and the upper body strength. I told him I was a basketball player and a baseball player."

"Did you think maybe he was kidding you?"

"Knute Rockne didn't kid. Not about football. He told me with my strength, he could make me a football player. It was very flattering, of course, but I was determined to become a civil engineer, and Purdue University was not far from my home."

After enrolling at Purdue University, he discovered at the end of his freshman year that engineering students were required to attend a camp every summer to put their classroom studies into practical application. As he had to work summers to help support his family, he had to withdraw from that program. So, like his brothers, he decided to become an English teacher. Had he known about the summer program when he originally enrolled he would have attended a university closer to his home, although probably not Notre Dame, because he wanted to be near the young woman he was courting, Nell Riley. His Nellie. "We went out once," he told me, "and I never dated another woman."

Purdue was where he became a national basketball star. It was a very different game at that time: It was played with a leather ball with a bladder stitched inside, and occasionally when the ball was dribbled it would take a crazy bounce, which led to a lot of passing. There also was a center-jump after each basket, which kept scores very low. Purdue's coach, Piggy Lambert, played a running game—he practically created the running game—which perfectly suited Wooden's aggressiveness and ball-handling skills. He was nicknamed "The Indiana Rubber Man," apparently because he was constantly diving for loose balls then popping right up off the floor. At Purdue, he became the first college player in history to be named a consensus All-American three times, and in 1932, when he led the Boilermakers to what was then considered the national championship, he was chosen the National Player of the Year.

As great a player as he was, though, he was far more proud of his academic achievements. There was a coatrack in the den of his condo, and among the numerous items hanging from it were the Presidential

Medal of Freedom, our country's highest civilian honor, which he had been awarded by President George W. Bush, and the medal he was awarded his senior year for being the Big Ten's Outstanding Student-Athlete. I could not tell you which of those two medals he valued more highly. After graduating, "The Rubberman" supplemented his income as an English teacher by playing professional basketball with teams like the Indianapolis Kautskys.

His coaching career began with a punch. Or, as he referred to it, "an unfortunate incident in which I overreacted." In addition to teaching high school English in Dayton, Kentucky, he was also the school's athletic director, as well as the football, basketball, track, and baseball coach. During an early-season football practice, a player challenged Coach Wooden's instructions. He openly defied the coach, daring him to respond. Coach's response was to punch him in the nose. The details are fuzzy, because Coach didn't like to talk about it. He was embarrassed by his lack of control and unchristian behavior. The most I ever heard him say was that it had been a mistake, and he regretted it.

But that was not the only incident of violence. While he was coaching at South Bend Central High School, his team faced off against Mishawaka High and their coach, Shelby Shake. After beating them for the second time, which hadn't happened in thirteen years, Coach

Wooden offered the traditional postgame handshake. To which Shake responded with "How much did you pay those officials?" Coach Wooden ran straight at Shake and threw a punch. Players and fans quickly grabbed both men to separate them. Coach Wooden and his team needed a police escort to their bus because there were Mishawaka fans waiting for them outside.

Coach was not averse to his players getting a little physical, either. In a 1941 game against Goshen High School, one of his players was pinched so hard by an opponent that his leg bled. The player wanted to go right after the pincher, but Coach told him to wait for the right time. A little later in the game, when his player was being guarded by the pincher, Coach gave him the nod. He faked in one direction, then shifted back. On his way back, he punched the pincher in the stomach as hard as he could. The boy doubled over. Somehow, the referees didn't see it. Neither Coach Wooden nor his player ever spoke about it, but when his player came out of the game, Coach gave him a pat on the shoulder.

Not the kindly, soft-spoken, fount of loving aphorisms that he later became.

I like to think about that story sometimes because it reminds me that, although we like to think of our heroes as perfect, the harsh truth is that they became heroes by making mistakes and learning from them. To me, that makes them even more heroic.

After his time as a successful high school basketball coach and three years in the navy fighting in World War II, he became head coach at Indiana State Teachers College. He won two conference titles there, and several universities offered him their head coaching jobs, among them the University of Minnesota and the University of California at Los Angeles.

This is one of those stories told about Coach Wooden that sounds like it came right out of a Hollywood screenwriter's imagination. When someone is described as a role model, this is the type of story that exemplifies that. This is one of those doing-the-right-thing episodes.

He really wanted the Minnesota job. He loved the Midwest, and he and Nellie wanted to live there, but he would only accept that offer if they allowed him to bring his own assistant coach with him. He also had visited UCLA and was unimpressed by the facilities; the cramped practice gym was on the third floor of an aging building, and the basketball team shared it with the gymnastics team. Home games were played in different gyms around the city, in high schools, civic centers, junior colleges. But UCLA agreed he could bring his assistant and offered him a two-year contract. When he insisted he required a three-year contract to move to California, they reluctantly agreed.

Still, he demurred. His roots were dug deeply in the Midwestern farmlands; Los Angeles was Hollywood and movie stars and glitz. He finally was forced to make his decision on an April evening in 1948. The University of Minnesota was scheduled to call him at six p.m. to tell him whether he would be permitted to bring his assistant. UCLA was going to call for his answer an hour later. Here comes the Hollywood twist: the lives-changed-forever event. For my father it was a missed audition for Count Basie's band; for Coach Wooden it was an unexpected storm. Minnesota didn't call at the scheduled time. Wooden assumed that Minnesota had lost interest, so when UCLA called right on time and formally offered a three-year contract, Coach Wooden accepted.

The phone rang again an hour later. Minnesota's athletic director was calling to apologize. A freak snowstorm had knocked down all the phone lines, he explained, and he hadn't been able to get through, but he was pleased to offer jobs to both Wooden and his assistant. But having given his word to UCLA, Coach had to turn down the job he really wanted. That was the way John Wooden walked through life. He had given his word. There wasn't any more discussion about it.

I'd already heard this story several times before I signed my first professional contract. It was part of the Wooden lore on the UCLA campus. I admired him for sticking to his word, but I never thought his story would relate to me in any practical way. Wrong again.

When I graduated, I was the first pick in both the NBA and the new American Basketball Association (ABA) drafts. I would either sign with the NBA's Milwaukee Bucks or the ABA's New York Nets. The idea of playing in New York was very exciting to me. The fact the Nets were part of a new league didn't bother me; I had seen what Joe Namath had done for the new American Football League. My negotiations were being handled by two Los Angeles businessmen I trusted completely, the well-known UCLA booster Sam Gilbert and a man named Ralph Shapiro, as well as my lawyer. We agreed we did not want to get involved in a bidding war, so we asked each league to make one bid. One take-it-or-leave-it bid. I knew the ABA needed me far more than the NBA did, so I expected to be playing in New York. And then the bids were made.

To my surprise the Bucks' offer of $1.4 million was substantially higher than the ABA offer. I accepted the Bucks' offer. Within hours we heard from ABA, telling us that was not intended to be a final offer. The new bid from the entire league was $3.25 million. I had no choice; I turned it down. I had given my word, I explained. I felt that the Bucks shouldn't be penalized for bargaining in good faith.

I wasn't consciously thinking about Coach Wooden when I made that decision. But Coach Wooden had been an integral part of my life for four years. He had developed my athletic skills, had nourished my intellectual pursuits, and had been a moral lighthouse that showed the way. My parents had laid a strong ethical foundation, but he had built upon that foundation, not just by showing how to determine the right thing, but by giving us the strength of character to *do* the right thing.

John Wooden was UCLA's fourth head basketball coach. At that time being UCLA's head coach was hardly a prestigious job. His annual salary at first was only $6,000. Basketball had not yet become a popular sport. The NBA would be formed a year after he accepted the job, when the Basketball Association of America and the National Basketball League merged. By far, the best-known professional team was the independent Harlem Globetrotters. College coaches were poorly paid, and if their games were broadcast at all, it was on a university radio station. Television barely existed. As part of his responsibilities as UCLA's head basketball coach, Wooden and his student managers had to sweep and mop the gym floor every day. "I carried the water bucket to dampen the floor," he laughed as he told me, "like I was feeding the chickens." He watered that floor every day for seventeen seasons.

After his second season in Westwood, Purdue once again offered him its head coaching job. The pay and the facilities in West Lafayette were considerably better than at UCLA—and it was Indiana, his alma mater, a chance for Coach and Nellie to go home. In addition,

UCLA had failed to fulfill its promise to improve its facilities, although, as he explained one afternoon, "It wasn't precisely a guarantee; it was more like 'an agreement.'" UCLA actually was willing to let him accept Purdue's offer, but reminded him that it was he who had insisted on a three-year contract, and they intended to honor it.

He had an out: UCLA had not fully lived up to its agreement. But he had given his word. That was stronger than any written contract. He turned down the offer from Purdue.

He was successful at UCLA. By the time I was being recruited in 1964 he'd had seventeen consecutive winning seasons. He had won or tied for eight conference titles, and the two previous seasons his teams had won the NCAA championship. Great players like Willie Naulls, Walt Hazzard, Keith Erickson, Gail Goodrich, and Kenny Washington had played for him. The "Indiana Rubber Man" was becoming the "Wizard of Westwood," one of the most respected coaches in the game. And finally, UCLA had raised the funds necessary to build that great arena he had been promised almost two decades earlier.

John Wooden had come to UCLA from the fields of Indiana; I came from the streets of New York. As I said, about the only things John Wooden and I had in common were a love of baseball and that big, round basketball.

When you are the tallest kid on your block, on any block in your neighborhood, you play basketball. I started playing basketball at P.S. 52 in Inwood, in Upper Manhattan. I was terrible. I had to heave the ball underhanded just to reach the rim. When I was only six or seven years old, I would shoot baskets with my dad. Actually, he would shoot, I would throw. He knew how to play the game. In high school he had been a teammate of Red Holzman, who later coached the Knicks to a championship. My father showed me how to play basketball, the hard way. He would push me around, elbow me all over my body until I was bruised and discouraged. He wasn't teaching me how to play; he was showing me who was boss. I had hoped it would be a way for us to bond. Instead, I never played with him again after that first "lesson."

For a time, baseball was my favorite sport. In eighth grade I was six-foot-eight and already throwing the ball over ninety miles per hour. I had a lot of velocity but no control—and more important, no one to coach me. I've always thought that I could have been a Major League player if only I could have solved that control issue. It was difficult for me to get the ball over the plate consistently. Everything with basketball came more easily. I really became fascinated with basketball when I was eight years old and saw the movie *Go, Man, Go!*, the story of the Harlem Globetrotters. There was a scene in that movie in which the great

Marcus Haynes dribbled past someone blocking him in a narrow tenement hallway. I saw that and I thought, wow, basketball is a pretty cool sport. Maybe that's the right sport for me to pursue.

My sophomore year at Power Memorial I made the High School All-American first team. No one could guard me well enough to keep me from consistently scoring, so I began to think basketball could be my future. By that time, I had learned how to be tougher. I remember we scrimmaged against Brooklyn's Boys High, one of the best teams in the city. What I didn't know was that my coach, Jack Donahue, knew several Boys High players, and before the game told them to rough me up a little. He wanted to see what I could take.

One of those players took it a little too far and bit me. Bit me! When I told that to Coach Donahue, he didn't believe me until I showed him the teeth marks. After the scrimmage, one of the Boys High players told Donahue, "You don't have to worry about that kid. He can handle himself."

Jack Donahue taught me the fundamentals of the game. Not the rules of the game, but the way the game is played. One year we went upstate to Schenectady to play Pat Riley's team. The officials fouled me out in the first half. I thought that was ridiculous; I wasn't a very physical player. Donahue explained reality to me: "They don't want us to win. You have to understand that. Your only friend on that court is the backboard. Sometimes the ball is going to bounce off right to you, and you'll get a rebound. But that's it." That was the start of my basketball education. It was how I learned to keep my arms up in the air and play without fouling.

Because Power was only a few blocks from the old Madison Square Garden, some NBA teams used our gym to practice. In return we were permitted to go to the Garden for games. Coach Donahue practically ordered me to watch the Boston Celtics' Bill Russell at every opportunity. This was at the time Wilt Chamberlain was setting every scoring record; he even scored 100 points against the Knicks one night. But as Donahue pointed out, while Chamberlain was scoring all those points, Russell's Celtics were winning all those championships.

No one had ever dominated the game defensively like Bill Russell. He eliminated his opponent's opportunities near the basket, forcing them to shoot from farther away, lowering their percentage. By denying lay-ups, blocking shots, and getting defensive rebounds, he allowed the Celtics to run and get quick shots. I was always a very capable offensive player, but after appreciating the value of his contribution, I worked on becoming a capable defender. Bill Russell became my template for how I should try to play defense. Donahue helped me build a strong foundation.

During my high school career, Power Memorial went 96–6; the 1963–64 team was considered the high school national champion and has been voted the best high school of the century. We had a seventy-one-game winning streak that was snapped by DeMatha High School in Hyattsville, Maryland, in what has been called the "High School Game of the Century." By the time I graduated, I had the raw tools to play basketball at a very high level. At that time, the NBA did not draft college-eligible players—there was no such thing as one-and-done—so wherever I went to school, I would be spending four years there.

Among those things that Coach Wooden and I did have in common was the belief that playing basketball wasn't the end, but rather the means to make our lives more fulfilling. I probably realized that when I was in seventh grade and I began receiving offers to attend the better Catholic high schools in New York tuition-free. That was when basketball first began paying some bills. Soon after that it became obvious that basketball would also pay for my college education. And I knew that professional athletes earned good salaries, so that too loomed on the distant horizon.

Colleges had begun recruiting me in tenth grade. At first I received a trickle of letters offering me a full scholarship at colleges and universities around the country, but gradually it became a flood. Even some universities that had segregated sports programs invited me to break the color barrier. Coach Donahue kept all the scholarship offers in a box in his office. I would stop there every week or ten days to see what new letters had arrived. Finally, so many offers had come in that Donahue told me not to bother checking the box anymore. "I can take this box and dump it in the trash. If any school has a basketball program that offers scholarships, you can go there." It was an overwhelming thought: I could choose to attend pretty much any university in America, and it wouldn't cost my parents a dime. All I had to do was play basketball.

Few young men have had as many choices as I did. I knew I wanted to go to a school where I could get a quality education while playing on a winning basketball team. I wanted a school that respected its students and athletes of any color or background, so that eliminated most of the schools in the South. I was eighteen years old; I wanted to go to school someplace where I could be away from my parents and have a good time. Eventually I whittled my choices to the University of Michigan, Columbia, St. John's, and UCLA. Coach Donahue had accepted an offer to become head coach at Holy Cross College in Worcester, Massachusetts, and told me I owed it to him to visit. I guess he thought the publicity would help his recruiting, although we both knew there was no chance I was going to go there. Holy Cross was a fine school, but it did not have a major basketball program. I wanted to play against the best competition. Out of respect for Coach Donahue, I made that visit.

St. John's was New York's home team. I had often gone to the Garden to watch them play. It was a nationally competitive, integrated program run by the greatly respected coach Joe Lapchick. In fact, when Lapchick was running the New York Knicks he had signed the NBA's first black player, Nat "Sweetwater" Clifton. I had met Coach Lapchick my freshman year at Power. Both he and Coach Donahue lived in Yonkers, and Coach Donahue worshipped Lapchick. We ran the St. John's offense; we watched St. John's games on film.

Coach Lapchick was six-foot-five, which was considered unusually tall when he was playing ball. I remember, as I was just learning how to be comfortable with my size, he told me, "I know what it means to be tall, Lew. Growing up in my old neighborhood, being tall was so unusual that little kids would point at me and say, 'Look Ma, a Gypsy.'" He meant that he was so startlingly different, that was the only way kids knew how to express their surprise.

Coach Lapchick was as much from the streets of New York as Coach Wooden was from the fields of Indiana. But they actually had played against each other in pro ball, when Lapchick was the center for the Original Celtics, who played in New York—and they'd gotten into a fight. "He kept pushing me," Coach Wooden told me many years later. Honestly, when he was talking about it he sounded like he was still offended by that. "The entire game, each time I went by him he would give me a little shove. Then, finally, as I was going by him to the basket, he stuck out his foot and tripped me. My goodness, I'd had enough of that. I jumped up and without considering the consequences, I grabbed him by the front of his jersey and threatened him, 'You do that to me one more time and I will knock your block off!'

"I don't know who was more surprised that I did that, him or me. If we had fought, I suspect it would not have been him who got his block knocked off!"

I remember when he told me that story I was laughing as I imagined the cartoon version of the fight: Coach Lapchick standing there with his hand on Coach Wooden's forehead, holding him safely at a distance while Coach Wooden continued flailing his arms.

Initially, I probably was more comfortable with Coach Lapchick: We were both New Yorkers, and playing for him appealed to me. But Lapchick had turned sixty-five the summer before my senior year and was pushed into mandatory retirement. I didn't know his replacement, a young coach named Lou Carnesecca, so that eliminated St. John's. Although I didn't attend St. John's, I did maintain a lifelong friendship with

Coach Lapchick's son, Rich. To this day, we still speak regularly.

In truth, attending UCLA had always been in the back of my mind. Many, many years later I found my grade school album. There was a page in the back about my future. In response to the question "Your Favorite College," I had written UCLA. That surprised me; I did not remember feeling that way about UCLA at that age.

I thought my interest in UCLA had begun in eighth grade, when I'd met Willie Naulls. Willie Naulls had played for Coach Wooden at UCLA and then became a star with the Knicks. I played in the Catholic Youth Organization All-Star Game, after which three Knicks, including Naulls, came up to talk to us. He kind of took me under his wing and told me it was a great place to go to school and that I would enjoy playing for Coach Wooden. "Coach Wooden's an unusual guy," he told me. "He'll make you better." He didn't say that he would make me a better basketball player, just that he would make me better.

As a kid I'd rooted for Jackie Robinson and the Brooklyn Dodgers, and I'd watched with dismay when the team had moved to the west coast. Robinson had played football at UCLA, where he was a star running back; at the time, UCLA was considered the most integrated college football program in America. My mother was thrilled when I received a letter from

Jackie Robinson—from the man she admired for his courage and intelligence—suggesting I consider UCLA. UCLA graduate Dr. Ralph Bunche, a black American who had won the 1950 Nobel Peace Prize and served as undersecretary-general of the United Nations, also wrote to me, suggesting UCLA would be a good choice for me. One Sunday night I was watching *The Ed Sullivan Show*. This was a variety show; each week Sullivan took a few moments to recognize and honor celebrity guests in his audience. On that night he introduced Rafer Johnson, a young black man who had won the gold medal in the decathlon at the 1960 Olympics, making him the greatest all-around athlete in the world. But what struck me was that Sullivan described him as UCLA's student body president. To me that meant that at UCLA I could aspire to be more than a jock, that the people there respected Johnson for all his abilities and gave him the opportunity to succeed. That was important to me. I didn't want to be categorized as *only* an athlete.

Also, UCLA had long been progressive. In the 1930s, the university had made the decision to be inclusive, even hiring a Jewish professor who had been blackballed elsewhere. And it had been that way ever since. During the recruiting process, the UCLA student newspaper, the *Daily Bruin*, wrote that one reason I should attend UCLA was that the university was well known for its "attitude towards Negroes." That actually gave me pause, since the word *Negro* had been replaced by Afro-American among progressives. But I decided their heart was in the right place, even if their vocabulary hadn't quite caught up.

So there were a lot of reasons for me to pick UCLA. But in the end the only one that really mattered was John Wooden.

There are two ways that a great teacher influences students: first, by the practical value of their words in teaching the student how to do things they couldn't do or can now do better; second, through the purity of their actions. Preaching moral platitudes is easy, but walking the line and living them takes great strength. Yes, Coach Wooden taught me a lot about basketball through his words. But more important, his example as a man of unbending moral strength taught me how to be the man I wanted to be—and needed to be.

Chapter 2

The Game Is Afoot

It's Never about Winning and Other Courtside Lessons

"A coach is someone who can give correction without causing resentment."

—*John Wooden*

The DVD player wouldn't work.

"Gosh darn it," Coach said, which is about as potty-mouthed as he got.

It was 2010, and we were sitting in his den just a few months before his death. He was ninety-nine. I had brought over the DVD of *Public Enemies*, the movie starring Johnny Depp as gangster John Dillinger. But something was wrong with the DVD player. The main reason I'd wanted to show the movie to him was for the music, which was from the 1930s, an era he remembered. Finally, after all these years, I wanted to explain my lifelong passion for jazz, which I didn't think he ever truly understood. I thought a gangster movie was a good way to ease into the subject.

At one time I'd had one of the most extensive jazz vinyl collections in the country, with more than five thousand albums. Then, in 1983, a fire destroyed my home and my precious record collection. Since then, thanks in great part to generous gifts from hundreds of basketball fans, my collection had not only been restored but surpassed the original. I was the resident jazz expert in this den, and I was ready to lay down some jazz truth on my old mentor. With or without John Dillinger and his blazing tommy gun.

"You have to listen to Billie Holiday," I said, holding up the DVD. "She sings 'Am I Blue,' 'Love Me or Leave Me,' and 'The Man I Love.' It will rip your heart out and serve it up gumbo style."

He laughed. "You love your jazz, Kareem. But I'm still a big-band kind of guy."

"Same basic music, Coach. Different sides of the same coin."

"'It don't mean a thing if it ain't got that swing,'" he agreed.

"Whoa, quoting Duke Ellington. I'm impressed."

He grinned to himself, like a man with a secret. "Son, you don't know the half of it."

"Do tell, Coach," I said, grinning back. "I'm all ears. Not as much as you, but still..."

He laughed. His giant satellite-dish ears had bloomed even more prominently as he'd aged. It was the only part of him that hadn't shrunk.

"Kids today," he said, shaking his head. I was sixty-two.

Coach leaned back in his big gray leather chair, which seemed to swallow him a little. "I was in Chicago one time in the thirties," he said. "About the same time this Dillinger fella was kicking up a fuss. We were playing at the Savoy Ballroom against the Globetrotters. After the game, Nell and I usually caught a train back to Indianapolis so we could be home as quickly as possible. Only for some reason this night we decided to stay in town a little longer. Remember, we were still in our twenties then."

I looked at the wistful expression on his pale, wrinkled face as he slipped through time to be with his wife again. As I'd gotten older, I'd learned just how devious aging was. When someone asked me how old I was, my first thought was thirty-five. Then reality shook me by the shoulders and I'd realize I was off by almost thirty years. Whenever I flipped on the bathroom light and suddenly saw my reflection in the mirror, it startled me. I always expected to see someone much younger. It was a crude form of time travel. Looking at ninety-nine-year-old Coach sitting there, his eyes slightly glazed behind his wire-rimmed glasses, I imagined he could time-travel through his memories with ease.

"After our game was over they took down the baskets, and the court we had just dripped sweat all over became the dance floor. All around the dance floor were dining tables. We grabbed a table and ordered dinner. The food was so good we stayed late and missed our train." He smiled at his own uncharacteristic spontaneity. "We had just finished up and were ready to leave when we heard some wild music starting up on the bandstand. Nell wanted to investigate. I was worried about catching the next train, but she insisted. She could be very stubborn."

"I remember," I said fondly.

"So, we worked our way to the stage, and there was Cab Calloway in a white tuxedo playing 'Kickin' the Gong Around.' Nell yanked me onto the dance floor, and we danced nonstop until two or three in the morning. I think we danced to every song."

"Were the other dancers mostly black or white?" I asked.

He dug back into his memory for a moment. "Black," he said.

I laughed, imagining Coach and his wife in their twenties, two of the whitest Midwesterners ever, kicking it with Cab Calloway and a throng of black dancers around them. He was still giving me lessons on poise, even now.

His story about Cab Calloway made me even more determined to help him understand why jazz had been so important to me my whole life. I fiddled with the DVD player, hoping we could still use the movie as gateway music to appreciating jazz. I have never been very mechanically inclined. All I could do was make sure it was plugged in and check the wires to the TV to see if they were snugly attached. They were. It still didn't work.

I looked around the den, hoping to find another DVD player he may have put on a shelf somewhere and simply forgot about. Given the massive amount of clutter, it was quite possible. I had been visiting this den for almost fifty years, and every time I saw something on a shelf that I hadn't noticed before. This could be where they stored Indiana Jones's lost Ark of the Covenant. The two main items that dominated the den were the dozens of framed photographs and awards hanging on the walls—and books. Books on the shelves, on the Shaker-style coffee table, on his rolltop desk, on side tables and lamp tables. The air itself smelled like old paper, the musty scent of a used-book store.

The rest of the space was filled with mugs, medals, plates, and souvenirs. There were bobblehead dolls and UCLA basketball jerseys and merchandise, there were basketballs from his five hundredth and one thousandth coaching victories and from his NCAA championships. His great-granddaughters' stuffed animal, Sheepie, was there, as were an American flag, stacks of videos, and one clunky nineteen-inch TV set that most often was tuned to a sports event or an old Western. He had the scorebooks from all the games played during his career. There were several different versions of the pyramid, as well as a stack of laminated cards, enabling him to hand a card to each visitor. I took some pleasure that on one shelf was the 1918 Lincoln commemorative fifty-cent piece that I'd given him because of his great admiration for our sixteenth president.

The long, comfortable couch and two easy chairs

faced the TV. An embroidered pillow on the couch quoted one of his heroes, Mother Teresa: "We can do no great things, only small things with great love." His old pool cue leaned against the wall in a corner. Every single item in the room had meaning to him, from photographs of each of his national championship teams to hand-painted plates signed by his grandchildren.

Nell had originally decorated it, but after her death he continued to fill it, maybe trying to fill the void she had left. He refused to change a thing, explaining, "There is nothing in this condo she didn't put up and so I couldn't take anything down."

I opened the DVD tray a couple times, not sure what I expected to find other than the copy of *Public Enemies* I'd snapped onto the tray. The only thing left to try was an exorcism.

"Let's watch some basketball, Kareem," Coach finally said, trying to save me from further embarrassment. "There's always a game on somewhere."

I found a college game between two schools neither of us cared about. We sat back and stared at the screen.

We watched as one player faked left and spun right around his opponent while bounce-passing to his teammate who was cutting to the basket. The first player then cut to the basket just in time to catch the second player's dish-off.

"Nice move," Coach said.

That gave me an idea.

"Have you ever realized that the way we played was a form of jazz?"

He looked over at me like I was crazy.

"It's true, Coach. You taught us to play basketball jazz."

He considered that for a few seconds, then smiled as if he liked that thought. "How so?"

Okay, Professor Kareem, you're up. After all these years, make it good. "Well, they both require a kind of structured freedom," I explained. "You didn't teach us to run set plays with diagrams and arrows. Instead, you taught us how to react to other players in the middle of the motion. We soloed here and there, expressed our individuality, but all within the framework of what the other players were doing. We soloed or played backup for another player, but we always played the same song, like a jazz band. We were playing in context."

"Playing in context," he repeated. "I like that. How long have you been preparing this lesson, Lewis?"

"Fifty years," I said with a grin.

"It's an interesting comparison," he said. "Certainly, doing anything well requires that individuals first master the fundamentals, then learn how to react as a group without thinking about it."

"Right. Did you ever read *Zen in the Art of Archery*?"

He shook his head.

"Bruce Lee told me about it back when he was working my butt off around his studio. It was written by a German philosophy professor who studied archery under a Zen master. Basically, the idea is that through years of practice, the archer no longer thinks about the bow, the arrow, or the bull's-eye because their body takes over unconsciously. Theoretically, a Zen archer is incapable of missing the bull's-eye."

"Like muscle memory," Coach said.

"Exactly," I said, my voice rising with enthusiasm. "Jazz takes place someplace beyond the conscious mind, that same place where great basketball is played."

And that's when it hit me, the bursting epiphany like the pop of old-time flashbulbs. I realized that, despite both of us liking strict structure in our lives, throughout our fifty-year friendship, Coach and I had been playing a jazz duet of friendship. He was the older, wiser master, blowing complex combinations of notes, and I was, and always would be, the upstart kid eager to learn but with his own song to play. The test of a true friendship was how many of life's tough obstacles you helped each other overcome—and we had helped each other through some really devastating times. We had each helped the other keep playing when he was too lost or too tired to continue. Sometimes you learn the most not through what a person says or even how they live their lives, but from where they are when you need them.

That day, just months before he died, we talked more about jazz and gangsters and basketball games. And we were both right where we needed each other to be.

It's where he had been since my first day at UCLA.

* * *

John Wooden stood in front of the greatest freshman team in the history of basketball. We sat on the UCLA bench awaiting the first words of wisdom from the coach we had come here from all parts of the country to follow. Some, like me, had turned down full scholarships at other schools just to learn at the feet of the great John Wooden.

"Good afternoon, gentlemen," Coach Wooden began dryly.

"Good afternoon, Coach," we chorused.

He looked at us all pleasantly and cleared his throat in preparation to speak.

We leaned forward, ready to tattoo his wisdom on our brains for eternity.

"Today, we are going to learn how to put on our sneakers and socks correctly."

Although we didn't dare snicker, we did look at one another as if wondering what the punch line to the joke was.

He bent down and took off his shoes and socks. His pale pink feet looked like they'd never been exposed to light before. "We are going to talk about tug and snug," he said. "Tug. And. Snug."

The 1965–66 freshman basketball team sitting on that bench included five high school All-Americans. I had graduated from Power Memorial in New York as the most highly recruited player in the country. My college roommate, Lucius Allen, from Kansas City, was already considered the best young player to come out of Kansas. Lynn Shackelford from Burbank, California, was an extraordinary shooter, and Kenny Heitz, from Santa Maria, California, was a confident, polished forward. Our fifth starter was Kent Taylor, a walk-on from Texas who later transferred to Houston. We had come to UCLA because it was the best college basketball program in the country, the perfect place for us to fully develop our talent before graduating to professional basketball. The Bruins had won two consecutive national championships during my junior and senior years in high school and were the preseason favorite to win a third during my freshman season, although they would have to do it without me and Shack, Lucius and Kenny. At that time freshmen were not permitted to play varsity basketball, under the NCAA rules.

This was the great John Wooden?

Snug-and-Tug Wooden?

We knew what he had accomplished, we knew that his program had produced great basketball players, and we were excited to learn from him. These were the first minutes of the first day of our four-year college career. We were eager to begin learning the techniques that had turned UCLA into a championship program.

Snug and tug was the secret to UCLA's success? I wondered, a little crestfallen. Well, we had come here to learn at his feet. We just didn't know that would be literal.

He grinned at our puzzled faces. "As Benjamin Franklin said, 'For want of a nail,'" he said, which only made us more puzzled. He sighed and recited,

For the want of a nail the shoe was lost,
For the want of a shoe the horse was lost,
For the want of a horse the rider was lost,
For the want of a rider the battle was lost,
For the want of a battle the kingdom was lost,
And all for the want of a horseshoe-nail.

He shrugged. "You want to learn about basketball, read Benjamin Franklin."

The greatest team in the history of basketball just stared.

"If you do not pull your socks on tightly," he said firmly, "you're likely to get wrinkles in them. Wrinkles cause blisters. Blisters force players to sit on the sideline. And players sitting on the sideline lose games. So we are not just going to tug. We are going to also make it snug."

He demonstrated. We copied what he did.

When we were done, he smiled and said, "For want of a nail, gentlemen."

We had entered the gym confident bordering on cocky and just gotten our first lesson in humility from

Coach Wooden. We knew that lots of teams started strong in a season, only to succumb to player injuries and drop out of the running. Any injury that kept you from playing hurt the whole team. It was that kind of attention to detail that helped make John Wooden the greatest coach in college basketball history. And none of us ever missed a practice or a game because of a blister.

He took a moment to make sure he had our full attention. He did.

"I don't drink and I don't smoke," he began, "and the only reason you have to be up beyond nine or ten o'clock is if you're studying." His Hoosier accent gave his words a nasal tone, but the intensity of his look gave the words biblical importance. "Number one in your life is your family. Number two is the religion of your choice. Number three is your studies: You're here to get an education. Number four is to never forget that you represent this great university wherever you are, whatever you are doing. And number five, if we have some time left over, we'll play some basketball." He raised his eyebrows. "Questions?"

There were none.

* * *

My freshman year at UCLA was difficult, just as Coach Wooden had warned. Back in New York, I'd had my own room, which had made me the envy of most of my friends. From the window of that room I would look out on the Cloisters, a museum constructed with elements from several French medieval abbeys surrounded by lush trees, and imagine myself climbing one of the towers with a sword and shield to fight alongside the Three Musketeers, just like in my favorite novel. If a beautiful, grateful damsel was involved, all the better, because fantasy females were the only ones I'd been experiencing lately.

At UCLA I suddenly was living in a dorm filled with strangers and sharing a tiny room with my teammate Lucius Allen, a bouncy kid from Kansas City, Kansas, with a "golly gee whiz" attitude about everything Californian. Definitely not like my boys from uptown back in New York. But, truth be told, there was something endearing about him. His unselfconscious enthusiasm was contagious. We became good friends and eventually played together for both the Milwaukee Bucks and the Los Angeles Lakers.

But that first day I was too numb to appreciate anything. As I walked down the hallway of the dorm, people would openly stop and stare at me. I'd grown used to that by now, but somehow I'd expected college students to be a little different, especially in California, where they were used to the unusual.

Most people think it's a great asset being tall, but there are some serious drawbacks that they don't consider. When you're six-foot-five in seventh grade, adults start treating you as if you're already an adult. They assume that height equals maturity, and they expect you to act accordingly. Be more responsible. Be more accountable. Be more like them. This continues throughout adolescence. I was only eighteen, but I stood seven feet two inches tall, which placed upon me some mantle of supposed wisdom and responsibility that I did not want. I wanted to be eighteen, be a freshman, be foolish sometimes. But I'd been treated for so long as if that sort of behavior were beneath me that I didn't know how to break out of it.

The other downside of enormous height is that I sometimes felt as if I were living in a parallel reality that existed slightly above where everyone else lived, and I couldn't find my way down to them. Imagine your head floating a full eighteen inches above most other people. They talk to you, but they also get tired of craning their necks upward. Slowly, conversations seem to be aimed at others whose eye levels are equal to their own. It was like a thin cloud layer separated me from everyone else. Size intimidates. Sitting at a restaurant table, my long legs tucked uncomfortably so others could squeeze in, I seemed to be taking more than my share of space. At apartment parties with everyone crowded in and dancing to a forty-five record of Smokey Robinson's "Shop Around," my head nearly grazing the ceiling, I seemed to be sucking up more than my share of the air.

None of this was deliberate, but it happened.

Which is why that first day I decided I'd had enough of being stared at and whispered about, and I marched straight to my dorm room, turned out the light, and went to sleep. My first Saturday night in California.

The next morning I was awakened by the phone ringing. I answered with a groggy hello.

It was the front desk giving me directions to the Newman Center, where Catholic mass was to be held. I thanked the voice, hung up, and pulled the covers back over my head. This was the first Sunday in my life that I deliberately skipped mass. I never went to mass again.

I felt a little guilty, for my mother's sake. She would be disappointed, and I hated to disappoint people. Lew Alcindor was nothing if not a people pleaser, a good boy that any young woman would be proud to take home to mama.

Or at least he used to be.

Briefly, I wondered what Coach Wooden would think. Everyone knew he had strong religious values. Did he expect his players to mimic him? Screw him, I thought, feeling pretty tough now that I'd made my first break from my past life. He was my coach and nothing more. I was here to learn basketball, and he was paid to teach basketball. I didn't need anything else from him.

Sometimes I wish I had a time machine so I could go back and kick my younger self's ass. Well, I would learn soon enough just how wrong I was about needing spiritual guidance.

* * *

Athletes were treated like movie stars at UCLA. But there was a hollowness to that fame, because most of us were broke. My scholarship entitled me to tuition and room and board, but it barely covered living expenses. Edgar Lacey, Lucius Allen, and I had come to UCLA with big reputations but nothing much in our pockets. We'd chosen UCLA for our futures, but that didn't make the present any easier. We were all cash-poor almost all the time. Worse, we were surrounded by students who were cash-flush, children of wealthy celebrities and business moguls who drove BMWs to their parents' Malibu homes. We barely could afford to go out on a date. We were part of a program that was earning millions of dollars for the university, yet I was literally wearing pants with holes in the pockets.

In our dorm room at night, Lucius and I dreamed of transferring to a school where they might be a bit more generous. We weren't really serious about it, just freshmen griping. Transferring to another school would have cost us a year of eligibility and, in reality, we would have faced the same restrictions.

I never discussed my unhappiness with Coach Wooden. We hadn't yet developed that type of relationship. I was on my own, shedding at least part of the identity that my parents had worked so hard to instill. And I hadn't yet figured out what to replace it with.

So I turned to basketball. I always knew exactly who I was and what was expected of me on the court.

* * *

What exactly did I hope to learn from Coach Wooden? I wanted him to somehow translate my relentless desire to be a great player and my hope to surpass even my own expectations into practical skills. Ball handling, shooting, setting picks, moving without the ball, teamwork. Check, check, and check. But there was something more that I wanted, something I couldn't articulate. I wanted the game to make sense in my life beyond just having a skill set. I wouldn't expect him to understand what I meant. He was old, an ancient fifty-five. He couldn't possibly get what was going on inside a young guy like me.

He wouldn't get the chance to understand, because my freshman team was coached by Gary Cunningham. Coach Wooden, who focused on the varsity team, didn't have too much to do with us. But we practiced each afternoon at the same time as the varsity did, with the gym divided by a large curtain.

"Why the curtain?" Lucius asked me one day as we ran warm-up laps.

"I don't know," I said. "Maybe he doesn't want them to see us and pick up bad habits."

"You mean like your turtle speed?" And he burst ahead of me. I ran after him. I was pretty fast for my size, but no one was as fast as Lucius.

At times I would look and see Coach Wooden peeking around that curtain, just standing there watching us. Some of the guys would pick up their game when they knew he was watching in an effort to impress him. I didn't change my play, because I always played as hard as I could. My parents had instilled in me a disciplined work ethic that dictated that I always try to work harder than anyone else in the room. I'd look over and see him studying us as if he were waiting for eggs to hatch, but it didn't make me nervous as it did some of the others. I was confident. Things were already going the way I wanted them to go.

Besides, I was studying him as hard as he was studying us. I respected his reputation, but this was four years of my life we were talking about. And whatever professional career I hoped to have afterward. I had to make sure that he wasn't a million dollars of promise worth ten cents on delivery. It wasn't arrogance, but self-preservation, survival. This was the only shot I would get, and I had to make it count.

Sometimes Coach Wooden would call over Coach Cunningham, give him some names, and a few of us would be sent over to work out with the varsity team. In part, he was helping us develop our skills. But he was also giving us a taste of what we could expect— if we stuck it out. We would be playing on an elite team that already moved with balletic precision but struck with SWAT-like force. The difference between practicing with the freshman squad and practicing with the varsity team was the difference between driving a Volkswagen and a Ferrari.

Practices were highly structured, scheduled to the minute, to the second, to the nanosecond. We knew that he spent two hours every morning just working out the schedule for that day's two-hour practice. He wrote everything down on three-by-five-inch index cards and kept a loose-leaf notebook with detailed notes of every practice session. Most other coaches would simply have pulled out their familiar list of drills that they used every year with every team. But Coach's philosophy was that teams were much more fluid. Other coaches saw their teams as a deck of cards. If one card dropped off, they just grabbed another card from the deck. The cards were interchangeable because they only looked at the backs of the cards. Coach Wooden looked at the face value of each card. No two cards were alike, just as no two players were alike. Even more interesting, he realized that a particular player was not the same player one day that he had been the day before, that each time one player progressed or faltered, the whole team's ability to read one another and predict what each would do was affected.

Sometimes he would climb to the very top level of the Pauley Pavilion, so high up you could reach up and touch the ceiling. And he'd watch us play from up there; we must have looked like a bunch of beetles scurrying around. Other times he would be courtside, walking along with the players as if he were our shadow.

I had never seen a coach think like that before. I had heard coaches talk about seeing the big picture before, but Coach Wooden saw the game in seventy-millimeter Panavision. Yet he also saw it on a microscopic level, too.

Every morning he scribbled on those note cards drills for the team and customized drills for individuals. I had never met anyone with such an eye for detail and such commitment to his players as names rather than numbers.

Sometimes my teammates and I would laugh a little about how focused he always seemed to be. Secretly, we also felt relief that he took our playing that seriously and wasn't willing to settle for anything less than our best. He saw his job as helping us find out how far we had to go to reach our best. Turned out it was farther away than any of us imagined. And a lot harder to get to.

Yes, he was driven to be the best coach possible, but he had no inclination to be our fatherly friend. He was our coach, and that meant he had a responsibility to each of us, a responsibility that was more a calling than a job. He not only dressed like a barnstorming Midwest evangelical preacher, he had the fervor for making us not just good players, but good men. We either didn't see that then, or we were so concerned with playing basketball that we didn't care.

But you can't shepherd impressionable boys for four years without you changing them—and them changing you. He may have started with the freshman team as the removed coach who was all about basketball, but his innate compassion kicked in, and soon enough he was less drill instructor and more Mr. Miyagi from *The Karate Kid*.

* * *

The biggest misconception people have about Coach Wooden is thinking that he focused on winning. It's an easy mistake to make, because he was one of the winningest coaches in history. But he didn't. In fact, he did the opposite.

"Asking an athlete if he likes winning is like asking a Wall Street broker if he likes money," Coach told us. "Sure, we want to win. I love winning. But winning isn't our goal."

I didn't say anything, but clearly this was sports heresy. People have been burned at the stake for less.

One of the freshman players raised his hand. "Coach Sanders says, 'Winning isn't everything; it's the only thing.'" He grinned a little, as if he'd just put one over on Coach.

Coach shook his head. Back in 1949, UCLA football coach Henry Russell "Red" Sanders had reportedly uttered those immortal words after a loss to USC. Immediately, coaches everywhere had used it as a mantra to whip up their players into a winning frenzy.

"Winning is the by-product of hard work," Coach explained patiently, "like a pearl is the by-product of that clam fighting off a parasite."

"I thought it was a grain of sand," someone else said.

Coach ignored him. Facts were facts. "The goal is hard work. The reward is satisfaction that you pushed yourself to the edge physically, emotionally, and mentally. It is my firm belief that when everyone on a team works as hard as possible until they feel that glow of satisfaction in their hearts and peace of mind, that team is prepared for anything and anyone. Then winning is usually inevitable."

To a freshman, this was crazy talk. Was the Coach having a stroke? Winning translated into attendance at games and alumni donations and television money; losing did not. His job and our scholarships depended on winning: That was a fiscal reality.

It took me years to fully appreciate this lesson. I'm pretty sure when Jesus first told his followers to turn the other cheek when someone smacks them, they probably said, "Say *whaaaat?*" They had to warm up to the idea. Even as a freshman I admired Coach's sentiment, even if I thought it was too esoteric. To me, you worked hard to beat your opponents. The satisfaction was in walking off the court with the fans screaming for your team, not theirs. But slowly, game by game, season by season, I started to see winning his way.

One thing that nudged me in his direction was witnessing how Coach reacted after a win or a loss, especially when the game was an important one. And they didn't come any more important than our January 20, 1968, game against the University of Houston Cougars, a match-up that everyone called "The Game of the Century." It was the first NCAA regular season game to be shown nationwide on prime-time television. We had played the Cougars the previous season in the semifinals of the NCAA Tournament and crushed them 73–58, going on to win the tournament. Because of our forty-seven-game winning streak, we were heavily favored, but we lost in the final seconds 71–69. I had the worst performance of my college career that game, shooting less than 50 percent. Of course, I blamed the eye injury I'd gotten at a game the previous week. The team was devastated. We were humiliated on TV in front of millions of fans. But Coach sauntered into the locker room, shrugged, and said, "Tonight they were the better team." No excuses, no blame. No running down the other team.

I felt a mixture of resentfulness and envy for him. My stomach was churning up inside as if I'd swallowed a barracuda and it was gnawing everything in sight. Coach looked fresh and chipper and ready to go another round. I wished I felt that way. He was going home and would undoubtedly fall into a restful sleep. I would lie in bed staring at the ceiling reliving every play, every point, every missed shot.

Neither the Cougars nor our team lost another game the rest of the season, which led us to a rematch in the NCAA Men's Division I Tournament semifinals. This time we destroyed them 101–69. We were jubilant in the locker room, celebrating our revenge. Coach Wooden came in, his expression the same as it had been when we'd lost. He congratulated us for a game well played. He made sure we acknowledged Coach Jerry Norman, whose diamond-and-one defense helped us contain the Cougars' top scorer, Elvin Hayes, who had been averaging 37.7 points a game, but that night scored only ten.

Coach walked out of the room, and I knew he was going home to another restful sleep. I would be up celebrating and later, lying in bed, reliving every play, every point, every missed shot.

Years later, I asked him about this. "Humble in defeat, modest in victory," I said. "You were so good it was almost annoying."

That surprised him. "Really? I hadn't thought about that."

"Yeah, you make the rest of us mere mortals look bad."

He laughed. "Believe me, Lewis, I'm just as mortal as the next fellow."

"If the next fellow is Gandhi."

He laughed again. "I always told you boys that winning wasn't the goal, trying your hardest was."

"Where did you get that notion? The Bible?"

He shook his head. "Kipling."

"*The Jungle Book*?"

"No, the poem 'If.' You know it?"

"Vaguely. We did it in English class in tenth or eleventh grade."

"It's a father's advice to his son. The second stanza is the key. 'If you can dream—and not make dreams your master; / If you can think—and not make thoughts your aim; / If you can meet with Triumph and Disaster / And treat those two impostors just the same.' At the end, he says that if his son follows these four stanzas of advice, 'Yours is the Earth and everything that's in it, / And—which is more—you'll be a Man, my son!'"

"Four stanzas of advice, huh. I think you've finally met your match." I liked to poke fun at his encyclopedic knowledge of writers and his ability to quote them whenever he needed to illustrate a point. An English teacher till the end. Ironically, this irritant eventually became my pearl; I became known in my writing for quoting various writers, poets, songs, and movies to illustrate a point I was making. When people ask me my literary influences, I guess I'll have to say Shakespeare, Langston Hughes, James Baldwin, and Coach Wooden.

"The lines I'm referring to, Lewis, are that Triumph and Disaster are the same. They're both impostors because they are momentary. More important is becoming a man of convictions. Lasting joy comes from that."

"In other words, win some, lose some."

He pretended to be exasperated, but he knew I was kidding him, as usual.

I said, "Doesn't he say something about filling every minute with running? I remember something about that."

"'If you can fill the unforgiving minute / With sixty seconds' worth of distance run.'"

"Like your practices," I said.

He laughed and nodded. "Like my practices."

It took me a while—okay, years—to get to the point where I could treat Triumph and Disaster as impostors. It's not an easy balancing act to maintain when your livelihood depends on winning. Toward the end of my career, I was able to sustain that perspective much more, walking off the court after a win or a loss with the same basic feeling that what had just happened was in the past and that I had played my hardest. After retiring from basketball, I began writing full time. Books, articles, movies, novels, and even comic books. Each was a challenge because I knew that there would be people out there criticizing, "Stick to basketball, Kareem." But I just wrote and rewrote and polished and then rewrote again, putting everything I had into every page. That process of trying my hardest was joyful. What happened afterward to the work, whether triumph or disaster, didn't matter as much.

The nice thing about having Coach as a lifelong friend is that whenever I wavered, he was there to remind me. And I like to think that I was there in his triumphs and disasters to lend a steadying hand.

* * *

Coach Wooden's Golden Rule of Basketball—and Life—was one short sentence: "Failing to prepare is preparing to fail." He borrowed that from Ben Franklin but he made it his own by applying it relentlessly to everything we did. Sometimes he said it loudly and sometimes softly, but he said it often, as if he wanted the words to seep through our skulls and into our brains in flashing neon lights. "Talent comes first," he said. "No one wins without outstanding talent—but not everyone wins with it, either!"

Talent only took you so far; preparedness took you the rest of the way.

One way he implemented this philosophy was through conditioning. Having just played on a national championship high school team, and being only eighteen, I thought I was already in great shape. He proved me wrong.

"The team that's in the best shape generally wins," he would tell us. "You want to know why so many games are won or lost in the last fifteen minutes? Because one team is out of gas and the other team isn't. We're always going to be that other team. Tired players miss more shots, defend less aggressively, snag fewer rebounds. That will *never* be our players."

And if anyone on our team dared to mention luck, as in "Man, that was a lucky shot" or "They just got lucky that game," he would retort with the inevitable, "The harder you practice, the luckier you get."

From the first day of my freshman year until the last practice of my senior year, we ran. And then ran some more. There were no shortcuts in John Wooden's basketball program. You did it until you did it right, and then you did it again. The basic philosophy that I learned on those long afternoons enabled me to extend my professional career to twenty years, longer than any other player. I always felt the conditioning regimen I was put through at UCLA was a primary reason I was able to play at a high level in the NBA far longer than players like Wilt Chamberlain. Wilt was dedicated to being stronger than anybody else. But he wasn't able to run the court, and he wasn't flexible. As he got older, things that required quickness and agility grew more and more beyond his reach because all he did was lift weights.

At UCLA practices usually were scheduled in the afternoon from two thirty to four thirty—which is why Coach said he wanted us to have short hair: It was cooler in the evening, and he was concerned that if we went outside in the cold with wet hair, we would be susceptible to colds and, as he pointed out, if we got sick we couldn't play, and if we couldn't play, we hurt the entire team. I didn't dare point out that colds were caused by viruses, not wet hair.

After practice I was so exhausted that I would have to go back to my room, collapse onto the bed, and take a nap until nine p.m. Then I'd wake up, do my homework until midnight, and go back to sleep. Not exactly the glamorous lifestyle that people imagined.

That strict regimen of endurance training paid off my first year in professional basketball. By the time I got to the NBA, I knew how to score and pass to my open teammate, how to block shots and rebound. But I had another ability I didn't even realize many of my teammates lacked. I had incorporated working to my fullest capability into my daily life. I never questioned it, I just did it. I was in better condition than any of the frontline players, and on a par with all of our guards. In the 300-yard run I was fastest guy on the team.

Early in my rookie NBA season we were playing in Cleveland, and I was the only one on the court really busting my chops. I scored thirty-seven points and had fifteen or so rebounds, I'd blocked some shots and had a couple of assists, but nobody else was playing hard. Our coach, Larry Costello, was furious. In the locker room after the game he chewed everybody out. When he got to me, he stopped, pointed at me, and said, "This is the only person out there that's working hard." As a rookie, I appreciated that shout-out because it meant I'd earned the respect of my teammates. I silently thanked Coach Wooden for pushing us so hard to reach peak conditioning.

We also practiced all the team drills Coach devised. And if he wanted one of us to work on something particular, he would pull us out of the drills for a few minutes and work with us. He didn't talk much during practices. Mostly, he taught us by demonstrating things himself. When he wanted us to move to a particular place, he moved us to that place. When he wanted us to make a certain pass, he showed us how to make that pass. We did our drills and we scrimmaged. The one thing he had no time for during practice was wasting time. We ran from drill to drill, station to station. If we relaxed for a moment, we heard it from him: "Come on, boys, let's go! If you're too tired to practice, you're too tired to play."

He had a rule that we were not allowed to drink water during practice. He gave us salt tablets to keep us from cramping. He never explained his no-water philosophy. Maybe he thought it would make us tougher, like French Foreign Legionnaires force-marching through the desert. Maybe he thought frequent water breaks would slow down practice. Whatever the reason, it was hard on us. Some players would sneakily suck on wet towels. But whenever possible, we would sneak to the water fountains. I remember telling him once how we would grab a drink when he wasn't looking or was distracted. I grinned at him slyly, proud at how we'd put one over on him. "Lewis," he said, "do you really believe I didn't provide those opportunities? You weren't my first team, you know."

Sometimes he worked just with me. I liked those private sessions because with each one I knew I was learning something that would make me a better player. The two of us must have looked a little incongruous;

this five-foot-ten-inch man stood next to me on the sidelines demonstrating the fundamentals of rebounding to his seven-foot-two-inch center. "Rebounding is positioning, Lewis," he emphasized. "If you are in the proper position, strength doesn't make a difference. All that contact around the basket is an effort to get the best position. Being quicker than your opponent to get that position negates his physical advantage." When he was teaching, he usually held a basketball in his hands and tried to look me in the eyes, or as close to my eyes as he could get. Somehow, when we did work on these things, the authority in his voice made him *sound* taller.

After we did our drills we scrimmaged. During a game, what often appeared to be spontaneous on the court was actually the result of hours of practicing until our responses finally became spontaneous and instantaneous. We didn't have any set plays. We had a basic offensive system—you go here, you go there, you go in that corner, stand over there—and then we would run several options off it, depending on how our opponents defended us. Our offense was structured to recognize opportunities as a group and take advantage of them.

We finished every practice by shooting free throws. We had to complete a one-and-one in order to leave. You had to stand there on the line shooting until you made them. And then, just before we left, he would remind us—the words were sometimes different but the thought always the same—"Just remember, everything we've worked so hard to get done today can be destroyed if you make a bad choice between now and our next practice."

The three top bad choices we could make were drugs, alcohol, and sex. Alcohol was a campus staple, an accepted tradition considered a benign way to blow off steam. But this was the mid-sixties, and drugs were flooding campuses around the country, helping to fuel the sexual revolution, both of which had risen in popularity too fast for Coach's conservative values. He was fighting a losing battle against the biggest cultural and political changes in American history.

Despite Coach's admonishment, some of us on the team smoked marijuana. I had been exposed to it back in New York and had occasionally indulged with my friends. At college, though, using it seemed hipper and more of a counterculture statement than just a way of getting high. Plus, it helped with my migraines, which were becoming more frequent. I also experimented with LSD for the first time, but quickly found I didn't enjoy the experience of feeling out of control.

Coach Wooden only got involved in our sex lives when he thought they posed a danger to us. And the main danger he saw was interracial dating. To Coach, interracial dating was a fairly recent phenomenon. He didn't realize how widespread it was on campus, especially among his own players. He spoke privately with Mike Warren, who was dating a white girl, and Kenny Heitz, who was dating an Asian-American girl, warning them of possible repercussions from outside. He never objected to the idea of interracial dating, but he had grown up in a place where the Ku Klux Klan would have responded to such a thing with extreme violence and worried about us coming to similar harm. He wanted to protect his boys, but he was out of touch with how rapidly the culture was changing. The Beatles had arrived. Civil rights marches continued. Anti-war protests had begun. Women demanded rights most people didn't realize they had been denied. Rebellion was in the air. Nothing could stop it, even a well-meaning coach.

Coach had a faith in the system that was charmingly anachronistic, like carrying a pocket watch or going on Sunday drives in the country. Even when he disagreed with the government, he believed they would ultimately do the right thing because people, even politicians, were basically good. At one of our team reunions, Bill Walton recounted how angry Coach was with him when he got arrested at a peace rally. Coach picked him up from the jail and drove him home, silently seething. Finally, Coach said, "How can you do this? You're letting me down. You're letting UCLA down. You're letting your parents down." When Bill expressed his anger at the war and how evil it was, to Bill's surprise,

Coach agreed. But Coach's solution was predictably quaint and polite. "Getting arrested is not the way to do it," he said. "What you should be doing is writing letters of protest."

To me, to Bill, to the students who played for Coach during this time, this was the same old line that those in power had been using for centuries in response to calls for social justice: "Wait your turn." Write letters. Strongly worded letters. We'll get back to you in due time. I'd been hearing that same response for years with the civil rights movement. "Due time" meant never.

Coach never brought politics to the team, but we brought it to him. He never discussed his beliefs with us, never asked us what we believed. He didn't care about what we thought, just about how we acted. Both on and off the court he expected us to reflect the values of fair play and respect for others. Unfortunately, the times were changing so quickly and dramatically that how to reflect those values was no longer as clear-cut as it had been.

People always ask me about disputes or disagreements I might have had with the coach. But the truth is that we were a winning team, and when you're winning, even if that's not the goal, you don't mess with success. If he'd told us to sleep with our underwear under our pillows, we probably would have. Instead, he pummeled us with preparedness to the point that we always felt confident when we faced an opponent that we were prepared for anything they could throw at us.

Practice did not make us perfect. We did lose two games during my four years there.

Coach Wooden's philosophy has proven to be a lifelong lesson for me. When I am scheduled to give a speech, I write it, then practice it, then practice it some more. When I write an article or a book, I research and research, then research some more. My opponent now is myself, my inclination toward laziness. The discipline I learned through those conditioning drills has allowed me to face my devious opponent and beat him consistently.

* * *

Coach emphasized teamwork over everything else. It was teams that won games, not individuals. A good team had room for individuals to rise, but their rise must lift everyone with them. That was the deal. No one on the team was a Robin to someone else's Batman. We were the Justice League, all with unique abilities, no one more special than the other.

That's why Coach hated to see showboating during practice. He didn't even permit us to dunk. Practice was a work session; we ran, we drilled, we scrimmaged. We didn't experiment with showy moves. Willie Naulls, who started for UCLA in the mid-1950s and had influenced me to come there, told me how he had to learn to play within the Wooden system. After he made a couple of no-look passes, Wooden told him flatly, "No fancy stuff out there." His teammate Johnny Moore pulled Willie aside and warned him, "Two hands on the ball will get you some playing time. Don't do your no-lookers, or you'll be on the bench watching me play." I took that advice to heart.

Guard Johnny Green, who played for UCLA from 1959 through 1962, had learned that same lesson after being reprimanded by Wooden. "Johnny is somewhat of an enigma to the coach," Wooden once told a reporter. "Watch the warm-up drill before practice. John will be out there trying to bounce the ball into the basket. I tell him that I don't really think that he's going to need that shot—and the next time he's doing something sillier."

Wooden may not have liked anything fancy, but he was flexible enough to appreciate when an innovation truly worked. A lot of basketball fans don't know that the lob pass was created at UCLA by Larry Farmer and Greg Lee. I think if they had done it first in practice with Coach Wooden watching, they would not have done it a second time. But it happened spontaneously during a game. Larry Farmer raced down the sideline on a typical UCLA fast break. That was our game. But this time, as the defense got set, he spun around his defender and, as he cut to the basket, Greg Lee, a world class volleyball player, lobbed the ball over the top of the defense as if he were setting an outside hitter for a spike. Farmer caught the lob in midair and laid it into the basket. It evolved right out of the basic offense; it wasn't planned, it just presented itself. "It was an aberration," Farmer explained. "We never talked about it, we'd never practiced it. There was no signal for it. We would make eye contact and do it two, three times a game. If it wasn't working, or the pass was intercepted, Coach would have nixed it. But it worked so well that finally he said one day, 'We probably should practice it.'"

It was jazz basketball at its best: a spontaneous combination of notes that rocketed the song to another level. The fact that Coach recognized innovation and was able to incorporate it showed that he was playing jazz with his team, not just conducting from the outside. As he often said, "Failure is not fatal, but failure to change might be."

The shot that really intrigued Coach was my skyhook. He always called it "Lewis's flat hook." A great professional player named George Mikan had popularized the hook shot in the 1950s. Those who mastered the shot liked it because it was so difficult to block. I was taught the hook when I was in fifth grade by a Manhattan College student named George Hejduk. I was at the St. Jude's grammar school, and my coach, Farrell Hopkins, asked him to work with the kids. "I got this kid, Lew Alcindor," my coach told George. "I can barely put him in the game. When he gets the ball, he fumbles it. He can't dribble at all, and he can't shoot." But there is a maxim in basketball: You can't teach height. I already was six feet tall; now all I had to learn was everything.

Hejduk taught me the George Mikan drill. As he described it, "I told Lew, 'Go to the left side of the key and take about two steps from the basket toward the foul line. Hold your hands up high; I'm going to throw you the ball. Just hold it there up high. I don't want you to lower it, I don't want you to dribble it. Just hold it up, step out toward the baseline away from the basket, look over your left shoulder at the backboard, and flick the ball off the backboard.'"

George and I worked at it for no more than a half hour, and only from the left side. From the very first it felt right. It was the first basketball skill I mastered. It didn't always go in, it didn't always hit the rim or the backboard, but I was diligent about practicing it. My friend Mike Kelley's father was the custodian at St. Jude's. He gave me a set of keys when I was in fifth grade so I could practice at night or when the gym was not being used. I had to be home before eleven, but between nine thirty and ten forty-five I would practice the George Mikan shot over and over and over. The movement came naturally; the ability to put the ball in the basket came with hours of practice. Done correctly, it is a graceful shot to watch, because it requires both rhythm and balance. Oscar Robertson compared it to a pirouette.

I got so good with it that when I was in eighth grade my friends Lefty and Pee Wee and I played George, Arthur Kenny, and Angelo Chiarello in Dyckman Park. They were all college-age players—and we beat them! George had done such a good job teaching me the shot that even he couldn't block it!

I worked on it for the rest of grade school and then for the rest of my career, going both left and right, and eventually without using the backboard. It was something I could do on the basketball court without looking foolish. Straight up, straight down. Nearly unstoppable.

Until I was in eighth grade I thought it was the greatest shot in the game. But when I was in eighth grade I dunked the ball for the first time. One day I couldn't do it, the next day I could. It was like one day I couldn't fly, then the next day I could. There is nothing graceful about a dunk. It's a pure power move, a smug display of dominance. I remember all the kids looking up at me with awe. *Lew can dunk the ball! Lew can dunk the ball!* After that, my step had a bit more swagger to it, as if the world and I had come to an understanding.

John Wooden did not like it, though. While he appreciated the result, he didn't like the aesthetic. Basketball was a beautiful game, he believed, and should be played with finesse. Years later he told a *Los Angeles Times* columnist, "If one of my players made a fancy dunk today, I'd put him on the bench." But in a bow to reality he admitted, "I didn't say how long he'd be on the bench."

My arrival at UCLA forced Coach to rethink a lot of his ideas. I was both an experiment and a catalyst for his own evolution as a coach. He had no experience with a player as big as me. "When Lewis arrived on campus, I have to admit I didn't know exactly how I could use a big man to the best advantage," he wrote years later. "I had ideas, but prior to this time I had no valid way to determine if they were sound or not. All the concepts that I believed would work with a big man needed one in order for me to find out." Trying to figure out how best to utilize me forced him out of his comfort zone as a coach. He had to improvise, innovate. He had to learn to play jazz.

He got his very first glimpse into what our future collaboration would bring when our freshman team opened the 13,000-seat Pauley Pavilion on November 27, 1965, with a game against the varsity. The varsity was favored to win a third consecutive national championship. In front of 12,000 fans we beat them easily, 75–60. We could have beaten them by a larger margin, but Coach Cunningham took out the starting team with more than four minutes left. After that, Coach Wooden wrote, "It was instantly obvious what Lewis could do and how he could dominate a game."

Coach Wooden and I met at my skyhook, or my flat hook, but either way, we worked on it like two mechanics perfecting an engine. It was that skyhook that brought us together on the basketball court. Working on it gave us the opportunity to spend extended time together. Both of us spoke fluent basketball, a language free of emotion. He loved that shot and saw in it possibilities I hadn't imagined. "It's an almost unstoppable shot," he told me. "If you can perfect it, it will enable you to dominate."

The dunk pleased the fans, but it required a certain flow of the game. The skyhook was mine. I could take it almost anytime I got the ball. We worked on every aspect of it.

By the time we were done, it had become one of the most identifiable shots in basketball history. I was in the habit of taking a couple of steps to enable me to launch into the air as high as possible. He worked with me to eliminate those extra steps, which enabled me to get the shot off faster. He moved me closer to the basket, so the ball would essentially roll off my fingertips. Finally, rather than sweeping it over my head in a high arc, he instructed me, "Keep the ball close to your body. I want your hand, your elbow, and your knee close and in line. I don't want you any farther than eight or nine feet from the basket, and when you get the ball, go straight up with it." That would make it more difficult for a defender to reach out and block it, and I could then shoot it with a straighter trajectory. "When executed properly, there is no way of defending that shot," he continually reminded me.

Executed properly was the key. We worked on it diligently in practice. The skyhook gradually got sleeker. As Coach instructed, I'd reach out with my left forearm to create distance from the defender in front of me, pivot, and launch myself into the air from my left foot, releasing the ball softly from my right hand and shooting down at the basket. He was right: It was virtually impossible for anyone to either prevent me from getting it off or blocking it.

It arrived at the perfect time. Prior to my junior season, the NCAA outlawed the dunk, declaring it was "not a skillful shot." That ruling, which most people referred to as the Lew Alcindor Rule, came as no surprise to Coach Wooden. In fact, initially he was concerned the NCAA was going to take more extreme steps to curtail UCLA's dominance of the game. And by UCLA, in this instance, he meant Lew Alcindor. Although I didn't know this at the time, he was fearful the NCAA might raise the height of the basket or, in a more extreme action, ban me from the game.

Toward the end of my professional career, I discovered that Coach Wooden had been among those who had voted to ban the dunk. I knew Coach's integrity too well by then to feel even a hint of betrayal. Even so, I couldn't help but ask him why he had done it.

"Coach, why would you vote to ban the dunk?"

He didn't hesitate. "I thought it was for the good of the game."

"Whose game? It hurt UCLA more than any other team."

He hesitated, then sighed. "It's an ugly shot, Lewis. Nothing but brute force."

That stung a little. I wasn't known for my brute force. To me, the dunk was all about timing and grace.

"The game is about teamwork," he added. "The dunk is about embarrassing your opponent."

We never did agree on that issue.

At the time of the ruling I was pretty upset. The entire NCAA had gotten together just to shot-block me. It was hard not to take that personally. Coach Wooden said publicly that it had been adopted after Houston players bent the rim dunking during pregame warm-ups in the 1967 NCAA tournament. No one believed that. Whatever the explanation, the reality was that dunking was no longer a part of my arsenal.

As usual, Coach Wooden took the most optimistic approach, telling me, "It doesn't make any difference whether you are or are not the reason. It's going to make you a better basketball player. You're just going to have to further develop the rest of your game."

At first, I didn't believe him. It was like telling Hank Aaron he was going to have to learn to bat left-handed. But my mistrust came from my own lingering anger at the ban. So what if I perfected my hook? Wouldn't they just ban that, too? Coach understood my disappointment, but he ignored it and kept working with me on my hook. His persistence in the face of my petulance built a closer relationship between us. I came to the realization that he wouldn't give up on me. I knew he wanted me to perfect the hook so I could be more effective in the games, but there was something in his attitude, a patient understanding, that made me feel that he was more interested in teaching me how to adapt to disappointment. To push through. To endure.

Coach taught me the techniques to hone the hook into my iconic shot that carried me through championships in college and the pros. But his real lesson about perseverance and adapting has carried me through life beyond the basketball court.

* * *

We were sitting in his den one Sunday afternoon in the late 1990s watching the NCAA tournament. I don't remember the teams, but a lower ranked team had upset a strong favorite and their coach was being interviewed after the game. He obviously was extremely proud of his team, telling the interviewer, "They gave a hundred and twenty percent!"

"No, no, no," Coach Wooden said. "Goodness gracious." Goodness gracious? This was serious!

Pointing to that coach on TV, he asked me, "Did you hear that, Lewis? That's just ridiculous. A hundred and twenty percent!"

Coach Wooden was not averse to employing sports maxims that met his strict standards. But there were some that irked him beyond all reason. Like this one.

"My goodness. Nobody ever gave a hundred and twenty percent. You can't give a hundred and twenty percent. Mathematically and physically impossible. One hundred percent is perfect, and you can't even get that."

"It's just an expression, Coach," I said, trying to calm him. "Why are you so fired up about it? If you want to picket sports clichés, I'd go with 'There's no I in team.' I hate that one."

As usual, he ignored me when I wouldn't play along with his rant.

"I was once on a panel in Boston with George Allen and Red Auerbach. Coach Allen was speaking, and he told us that he always demanded one hundred thirty percent from his players. So I raised my hand, and when he called on me, I asked, 'Coach Allen, how in the world did you manage to get one hundred thirty percent out of your players?' He asked what I meant. I explained, 'I was never able to even get a hundred percent out of any individual. I just tried to get as close to it as possible. So I was wondering how you got a hundred thirty percent.' He thought about that for a moment, then replied, 'Coach Wooden? Please sit down.'"

I was silent a moment, then said, "There is a 'me' in team, though."

He looked at me a long moment, then laughed.

Right there, that laugh, that ability for him to laugh at himself, at me, at the silliness of coaches demanding 130 percent: That was what I loved about this man.

Chapter 3

Color Bind

The Unbearable Darkness of Being Black

"Am I not destroying my enemies when I make friends of them?"

—*John Wooden*

The most awkward and uneasy part of my relationship with Coach Wooden had to do with race. On the court, there was a smooth rhythm between his coaching and my playing. Over the decades of our friendship, there was an effortless flow of respect and affection between us. We were like synchronized swimmers or musical theater dancers. But when it came to race, we just couldn't find a comfort level. We were itchy and fidgety. During my four years at UCLA, we faced racists together, we discussed the plight of black Americans, and we dealt with racial hostilities among fans. But that didn't bring us closer.

He didn't quite understand that when you're black in America, everything is about race.

That may seem like a provocative sentence to those who aren't black, but that's because they haven't had to face the consequences of being black every day of their lives. They witness the devastating effects of racism as a diluted reflection through the hoary lens of television, partisan radio jocks, and newspaper articles that distill people's daily horrors into five column inches.

To African-Americans, white America lacked awareness of the problems, lacked compassion to find out about the problems, and lacked interest in fixing the problems. It was like the scene in *Hidden Figures* when the distant white boss of women workers at NASA tells black Dorothy Vaughn, whose life she had been making miserable, "I have nothing against y'all." To which Dorothy responds, "I know." Then she adds with a smile, "I know you probably believe that." Many white Americans then didn't see themselves as racist because they hadn't done anything directly harmful. But, as Coach Wooden had said in another context, quoting British politician Edmund Burke, "The only thing necessary for the triumph of evil is for good men to do nothing." Good people were doing nothing, and evil sure seemed to be triumphing. At least in black neighborhoods.

Especially in 1965, when I was a freshman at UCLA.

The few months leading up to my attending UCLA were filled with enough racial violence to make us wonder just how long ago the Civil War had been. That February, a peaceful march had ended with a state trooper, James Bonard Fowler, killing an unarmed black protestor, Jimmie Lee Jackson, age twenty-six, while he hid with his mother in a café. Three days later, members of the Nation of Islam assassinated

Malcolm X, a man I greatly admired. Two weeks after that, what became known as Bloody Sunday occurred. In Selma, Alabama, John Lewis led about six hundred civil rights marchers across the Edmund Pettus Bridge, where they were met by hundreds of state troopers, most of whom had been deputized that day when the county sheriff had sent out a call for all white men over the age of twenty-one to report to the courthouse to be sworn in. The troopers, some on horseback, attacked the marchers with nightsticks and tear gas. Within the next month, Dr. King led 2,500 marchers in Selma across the same bridge. That night Ku Klux Klan members beat three ministers, one of whom died. Just a couple weeks before I started classes at UCLA, Los Angeles had its own taste of race riots. Protests over police brutality escalated into full-blown rioting in the predominantly black Watts section of Los Angeles. The violence lasted for five days, with 34 people killed, 1,032 injured, 3,438 arrested, and more than $40 million in property damages.

By this time, I had a few life-changing experiences of my own: I had interviewed Dr. Martin Luther King, Jr., I had been caught up in a racial violence in Harlem, I'd had my childhood best friend scream "Nigger!" in my face, for starters.

I hadn't come to California to play basketball so I could escape the racial divide that was tearing apart the country. I'd come to learn more about myself, to find my voice, to figure out what I could do to help. I was primed to join the fight, but I didn't yet know what form my fighting would take.

The reason I was so unsure of myself had nothing to do with the issues that we black Americans faced. I was rock solid in my commitment to supporting voters' rights, anti-poverty programs, civilian oversight of police departments, and many other items on the civil rights agenda. My personal issue was because I was still a little tender after the betrayal I had experienced a little more than a year before. It had shattered me on a personal level, making me wary and suspicious.

Jack Donahue was my coach at Power Memorial Academy, a ten-story brick building that had once been a children's hospital but now was a Catholic high school. I excelled academically as well as athletically, but the racial tidal wave washing over the country had seeped into this bastion of traditional values. I was one of only a dozen black kids out of about nine hundred students, and many of our white classmates, having never been around black kids, viewed us with condescension. To them, thanks to their fretful parents informed by conservative political pundits, all blacks were ticking time bombs on a countdown to an inevitable explosion. We were all Nat Turners just waiting for our chance to take over the plantation and pitchfork our way to freedom.

The teachers were no better. They followed a curriculum that omitted all mention of black inventors, scientists, writers, artists, and politicians from our studies, so it was no wonder students were surprised at my use of logic and my ability to debate in class. I had white friends and white teammates, but a large part of the student body chose to actively ignore me. I reacted in kind.

My skin made me a symbol. My height made me a target.

I found solace and purpose in basketball. My new coach was only thirty years old and was enthusiastic about me being on the team. I was raw, with more desire than skill, but I was six feet eleven inches tall at fourteen years old. He patiently taught me the fundamentals until our team dominated New York City. He was a tough taskmaster, not afraid to raise his voice or sling sharp barbs at us if he didn't like the way we were performing. But he also picked me up sometimes and drove me to school, during which time we would sometimes chat about life. He also took me to Madison Square Garden to see professional basketball games, making sure I saw Bill Russell and Wilt Chamberlain in action.

"That could be you some day, Lew," he said.

"Yeah, right," I said, trying to sound modest. But secretly I didn't think I *could* be like them, I knew I *would* be like them. Maybe better.

"You just keep learning like you are now, and I guarantee it. You'll be playing right here in the Garden someday."

Someday. To a kid, those words seemed a long, long time away.

But I had faith in Coach Donahue. He'd snatched me out of the freshman team and put me on the varsity team, a rare honor. He'd even given me a jersey with my favorite number, 33, in honor of my favorite football player, Mel Triplett, of the New York Giants. Even though I got off to a rocky start on the team, eventually it all came together, and we were unstoppable.

I'd never seen anyone who wanted to win as much as Coach Donahue did. At UCLA, I would often ponder the differences between Donahue's and Wooden's styles and attitudes. Donahue was of the scorched-earth philosophy. He believed embarrassing and ridiculing us and making fun of us was the fuel that drove us as a team. Wooden believed that pride in one's performance coupled with loyalty to your team was the fuel.

Despite the barbs and the yelling, the snorts of frustration, the sighs of disappointment, I believed Coach Donahue cared about me, and so I gave him all I had. In my sophomore year we won the city championship, which the school hadn't won since 1939. The players were heroes at school. Those students who had ignored me before were willing to be much more cordial to me now. But I didn't want it. My only worth to them as a human being was that I brought a trophy to their school, which made our victory kind of hollow to me. I had done something to make them proud, which seemed like a betrayal of my people.

Coach Donahue's attitude about racism seemed enlightened to me, which made me like him even more. During our drives to school, he would tell me about the terrible racism he had seen in the army while stationed at Fort Knox, Kentucky. He believed that the only way racism would end is by each new generation becoming less racist until it just disappeared. While I appreciated the thought, I couldn't help but think how many generations had lived in this country, yet still there were segregation, lynchings, murder, denial of voting and jobs. How many more generations would it take? And why should we have to wait? Would he wait if it were his children being discriminated against?

During the summers I would attend Coach Donahue's Friendship Farm basketball camp. At first it was just one building built in the 1780s and a dirt court, but each summer he made improvements. Apparently, I was something of a draw for the camp because of our city championship.

By my junior year not only were we winning all our games, but the scholarship offers had begun pouring in. My parents trusted Coach Donahue to guide us through the offers to make the best choice. When he told me that I could attend any school I wanted on a full basketball scholarship, I was ecstatic. Any school! If this man could deliver any school to me, I would work even harder for him.

One afternoon we were about to play St. Helena's, a Catholic school in the Bronx. We were undefeated, and this school didn't have much of a team. We were all confident we would make quick work of them. The only problem was deciding how many points we would beat them by. But when the halftime buzzer sounded we were up by only six points, which in basketball can be erased in thirty seconds.

We filed into Coach Donahue's cramped office with our heads hung low, knowing we were about to get a world-class tongue lashing. He closed the door and began to rage.

We didn't deserve to win.

We were sleepwalking.

We were terrible.

A disgrace.

We stared at the floor, watching our sweat drip by our sneakers. We didn't disagree.

But then he turned his anger on me. He pointed his finger at me as if it were a dagger he wanted to jam into my chest. "And you, Lew! You go out there and don't hustle. You don't move. You don't do any of the things you're supposed to do." His eyes flared. "You're acting just like a *nigger*!"

Some essence drained out of my body. I couldn't have gotten out of my chair even if the building were on fire. My face burned as if I'd been repeatedly slapped. My heart felt as if it had been crushed into a walnut. Not since my ex–best friend had yelled "Nigger!" into my face had I felt so betrayed. I was angry, sure, but I also felt worthless, as if I had just been discarded into the trash by someone I cared about.

Somehow I played the second half. Somehow we won. Somehow I didn't care.

After the game, Coach Donahue pulled me into his office. He was jubilant.

"See!" he said, grinning from the edge of his desk. "It worked! My strategy worked. I knew that if I used that word it'd shock you into a good second half. And it did!" He beamed at me as if we'd just won the father-son sack race at the school picnic.

He kept talking. About how clever he'd been in motivating me. About how we were going to beat the next team. How it was up to me to keep the fans from looking at me like the stereotype of a lazy nigger, so I would have to work even harder. He seemed to believe he was my race savior.

When I got home and told my parents, they were livid. They felt as betrayed as I did. This was the man to whom they'd entrusted their son's future. In my anger, I insisted on switching schools immediately.

How could I continue to play when every victory would also be a victory for the man who had just called me a nigger? But as I calmed down, I realized that in changing schools I would lose a year of eligibility and would take an extra year to graduate from high school.

I went back to Power Memorial. Back to Coach Donahue. Even back to Friendship Farm. Being in his presence that whole year made me feel like I was always short of breath, like my chest had been wrapped too tightly with an Ace bandage. But it didn't affect my playing. In my senior year we lost only one game and were chosen national champions for a second year. I made All-City and All-American.

And I made UCLA.

It was because of the fresh scar of Coach Donahue's betrayal that I kept myself a little aloof from Coach Wooden. I had been trusting once and had my heart broken. I wouldn't let it happen again. I couldn't afford to. I would force myself to be wary, especially of older white men pretending to be my friend.

Years later, after Coach Wooden and I had become close friends, he told me a story about Coach Donahue he hadn't told me before. In 1965, after UCLA had won its first national championship, he'd appeared on television. Shortly afterward, he'd received a phone call from Jack Donahue. "I see you're speaking at a coaching clinic in Valley Forge, Pennsylvania," he'd said. "I'd like to come down and talk to you about my player, Lew Alcindor."

"Well," Coach said, "he came down and told me that UCLA was one of the four schools you wanted to visit. That was the first contact that we had with you. Did you know that?"

"No," I said.

"Long drive," he said.

I didn't say anything.

"Two and a half hours," he said.

"Has anyone ever accused you of being too subtle?"

He laughed. "Quite the opposite. I'm accused of cranking out neat little sayings that are t-shirt ready."

I laughed, but I got what he was saying. What kind of man drives five hours to help a kid who barely talks to him and never tells the kid he did it?

"Have you ever made a mistake, Lewis?" he asked me quietly.

Shot taken. Point scored.

A few years after that conversation, I was at his house watching women's basketball. He was a huge fan because he liked the way they executed the fundamentals so well.

"No showboating," he said, "just great ball handling and shooting."

"I think you just like the shorts," I teased.

He just shook his head. "Kareem, what am I going to do with you?"

"Put me in your will?" I suggested.

That made him laugh.

The phone rang before he could snap out a comeback. It was Coach Donahue. He was in Los Angeles and wanted to visit Coach Wooden. By this time I didn't really have any animosity left, so knowing he was on the other end of the line didn't really bother me.

"I've got someone here I'd like you to talk to," Coach Wooden said and handed me the phone.

I took the phone. "Hey, Coach," I said cheerfully. "How are you?"

"Fine, Kareem, fine." I could hear the relief in his voice, and I was glad.

We chatted briefly, made arrangements to meet in a couple hours, and hung up.

Coach Wooden looked at me appraisingly. "You good?"

"Try to be," I said.

He chuckled and shook his head again. But he wasn't chuckling at my lame joke, he was just pleased that I had done the right thing. And I was pleased that Coach had somehow arranged this "coincidental" call. He knew how much it had bothered me in the past and wanted me to have closure. Even more, though, I think he sympathized with Coach Donahue and the heavy burden he'd carried all this time. As a coach, Coach Wooden knew how easy it was to make a mistake in the heat of competition, and how hard it was to recover from that mistake.

I met Coach Donahue at my home. He apologized again, as he had done to me and in the press when the story came out. Since then, he'd gone on to a distinguished career, including coaching four Canadian Olympic men's basketball teams. It touched me that, despite all he had accomplished, he still was bothered by how he'd hurt a seventeen-year-old kid thirty-five years before.

I told him I forgave him, that I had realized within the week that he wasn't a racist. He had just unknowingly been insensitive and overreacted, which was easy to do around a kid so cocky and full of himself as I had been. I thanked him for all he had done for me, which he looked grateful to hear.

My dad, who was living with me at the time, came out with a bottle of Bushmill's Irish whiskey. He wanted us all to have a drink together, which we did.

We parted with a handshake and good feelings toward each other. Eighteen months later he died of prostate cancer. I attended his memorial.

It was appropriate that Coach Wooden had brought us together, because it was his example of kindness and compassion that helped me become the kind of man who could let go of animosity and forgive past hurts.

* * *

Then came the evening that would change our relationship forever.

To celebrate our undefeated season, Coach invited me to dinner for some one-on-one time. We both knew that the fans and the press had a lot of expectations for both of us in the next three years. He had kept me away from the press all year, just as Coach Donahue had, in an effort to protect me from being distracted. But that was about to end, and he wanted to make sure I would be able to handle the inevitable criticism that came with the praise.

"The press has made you a hero," he said to me as we pulled into the parking lot of the restaurant. "And that feels pretty darn good, right?"

"Sure," I said. *Oh man, did it ever.* Seeing my photo in the newspapers and sports magazines, reading all the great stuff they said about me, that was a dream come true.

"Well, they can turn you into a villain just as quickly. They don't like something you said, or didn't say. They think you snubbed them or dodged a question." He shook his head. "They can turn on you."

Coach had faced some criticism and questioning of his own this past season when his team failed to make the NCAA Tournament. Our fortunes were now bound together and we would rise or fall together over the next three years.

COACH WOODEN and ME • 129

Coach and I were both huge baseball fans, so he took me to a steak house called the Bat Rack. The owner, Johnny Sproatt, had decorated the place with baseball bats signed by Major League players. We ordered and settled in for some light conversation. Despite the fact that the country outside this restaurant was in racial upheaval with riots, murders, and marches, Coach Wooden and I didn't talk race, we talked baseball and basketball. He had carefully constructed a cocoon around his players designed to keep the raging storm silently outside.

I looked around the restaurant at all the autographed bats hanging from the walls. In some ways, this was the most appropriate restaurant for our relationship. Our bond was sports, and sports was a fantasy. Basketball was an artificial world or rules, regulations, mutual respect, and civilized behavior. The real world outside was a live volcano of violence and racial injustice. Right now it was spitting out ash and hot embers, but we could all hear the rumbling of boiling lava on the verge of eruption. It wasn't a matter of if, but when.

I hadn't made up my mind yet about where Coach stood in all this social upheaval. I liked him. I admired him. And, until he did something like Coach Donahue, I would listen to him and do what he advised. And I would eat the steak he was paying for.

After dinner we stopped on the way out to say hello to the owner, Johnny Sproatt, who was a major UCLA booster. While we were standing there talking, an elderly white woman came out of the restaurant and just stood there, staring up at me. She reminded me of Granny in a popular TV show, *The Beverly Hillbillies*. I was used to people gaping at my height, so I just smiled at her politely.

Finally, she asked Coach Wooden, "How tall is that boy?"

"Seven foot, two inches, ma'am," he said.

She considered that for a few seconds, then shook her head and said, "I've never seen a nigger that tall."

I didn't react. I looked down into her wrinkled, grandmotherly face and could tell that she had no idea that she was insulting me. To her, nigger was the same as saying Negro, or Afro-American, as was being popularized back then. Confronting her would have been a waste of time. Plus, there's no upside to a seven-foot-two-inch black man yelling at a five-foot-two-inch-tall old white woman.

But Coach Wooden did react. His whole body stiffened; his cheeks reddened. He looked at the old woman incredulously. He didn't know what to do, how to respond. This was not his world. We had stepped out of his cocoon.

Mr. Sproatt was waving to another customer just arriving. He had not heard the woman—or he was pretending not to have heard her. Coach looked up at me, clearly hoping I hadn't heard her. But when he looked into my eyes, he knew I had.

Over the years, I often thought back to that moment and tried to see it from his perspective. Did he wonder if I expected him to say something, to come to my defense as my coach, as an adult, as a white man? He had to be having a crisis of conscience: Go against his Midwestern morals by shouting at an old lady who wouldn't really understand his anger. Go against his Christian values by not standing up for a young boy who had been deeply insulted. Go against his patriotic values and not condemn her un-American racism.

In the end, he said nothing to her, and she just walked away, never aware of the emotional chaos she had left in her doddering wake.

On the drive back to campus we both stared straight ahead at the road, unwilling to look each other in the eyes. Finally, he broke the uncomfortable silence. "You know, Lewis, sometimes you take people by surprise. Someone your size, it startles them."

"Uh huh," I muttered, not sure where he was going with this.

More silence. He was carefully choosing each word. "Sometimes people will say things they don't mean or don't really understand. Please don't think all people are like that woman. Don't let ignorant people prompt an ignorant response from you. I know it's difficult, but let's not condemn everyone for the actions of a few."

Was he talking about her or himself? About what she said—or what he didn't say?

"Sure, Coach," I said. I didn't really want to talk about it. What was the point? There was nothing he could say that I hadn't heard before, mostly from well-meaning white people. I was used to it so it was no big deal, but I could see it was eating him up. I didn't want that. I could see that he was a good man, and I was touched that this incident was tearing him up so much inside.

We didn't talk about it again, but Coach never forgot that night. Interestingly, when he recalled that night when speaking publicly, he remembered it differently than I did. In his memory, the woman said, "Will you just look at that big black freak?" The word *nigger* was too painful to even store in his memory, and maybe it lessened his guilty feelings a little.

It wasn't until years later that I realized how deeply that encounter had affected Coach. When he told his close friend, the great LSU Coach Dale Brown, about it, he said reflectively, "That really opened my eyes to things. I tried to become a lot more sensitive to stuff like that. My heart went out to Lewis. I thought, this is what he has to live with every day, and yes, my heart went out to him."

Nothing seemed to change between us after that night. He coached, I played. We didn't discuss race, he didn't ask me how I felt about what was happening, I didn't give him copies of *The Autobiography of Malcolm X*. But there was an unspoken difference. We were inexorably bound together by what had happened that night. We had glimpsed into each other's hearts, and that connection had shoved us beyond the coach–player relationship.

* * *

When it came to racism, I thought Coach Wooden had a good heart, but he was on the sidelines in this game. It wasn't happening to him, only around him. But for me, it was part of my daily life, as Coach Wooden soon saw for himself.

I had received national publicity while I was still in high school, but it exploded when I began playing at UCLA. After playing only a few games my sophomore year, the student newspaper, the *Daily Bruin*, suggested they change the meaning of the UCLA initials from standing for the University of California at Los Angeles to standing for the University of California at Lew Alcindor. Flattering, sure, but also a little scary, because now I was a target for rivals' anger.

The first time we played against UC Berkeley, I could hear a lot of the Berkeley fans shouting "Hey, nigger!" and "Where's your spear?" Variations on that theme generally combined "nigger" with a choice profanity. There's very little creativity in racism. That was standard operating procedure at most games. I knew that the fans were trying to knock me off my game, so I chose to ignore their comments and give my response on the basketball court. Of course, beating their teams game after game only increased their racist taunts. The racism was so prevalent that even reporters began to ask me whether these comments made me bitter toward the fans. "Bitterness gets in your way," I told them. "You get involved in revenge instead of trying to create a change. I used to be bitter, but now I just play hard to win."

That was my official response. It reinforced Coach Wooden's creed. "Revenge is something I don't harbor," he said. "I believe if I don't harbor it, my boys won't harbor it." I was being a team player. But inside, there was no way having people call you nigger every night doesn't affect you. I fought it. I wanted to be the good person, the evolved person that Coach wanted me to be, not just for him, but because I thought it would bring me some peace. But it was hard, sometimes too hard for a teenager. For his sake, for the team's sake, for my sake, I fought the bitterness.

Eventually, bitterness turned to a form of triumph. One evening in 1967 in Louisville, Kentucky, Coach and I were returning to the hotel after having dinner. We had just defeated the University of Dayton in the Finals. As we neared our hotel, we could hear people shouting down at me: "UCLA sucks!" "Go home, nigger!" Instead of feeling anger, I grinned with satisfaction that our playing had made them this hostile.

"Nothing we can do about their ignorance, Lewis," Coach said.

I agreed. Besides, I'd already delivered my presentation of racial equality earlier that evening when we crushed their team.

Louisville had always been particularly aggressive racially during those years. But when I visited the city's Muhammad Ali Center years later, I was pleased to see how much the city had changed.

For a time, Coach Wooden ignored the remarks or acted as if he didn't hear them. As long as there was no direct confrontation, he didn't have to address it. But that changed one night. After a game, Coach Wooden and I usually were the last people out of our locker room. I was kept late doing interviews, and Coach stayed to make sure the locker room was clean. Some thought it was amusing to see the winningest coach in college basketball picking up trash from the wet floor, especially after a victory. But I found it moving, not just because he was conscientious enough to want to leave the room as clean as we'd found it, but because he was humble enough not to think it beneath him to do it himself. However, I always suspected that the real reason he hung around so late was to watch out for me during those interviews without seeming to. Knowing he was there gave me more confidence to speak my mind, but also reminded me that there was grace in modesty. He was making me a better person just by walking around grabbing wet towels from the floor.

As we left the locker room after our game against Oregon State up in Corvallis my sophomore year, I stopped to sign autographs for a group of kids who had been waiting outside in the brisk night air. I had probably signed thirty or forty when Coach told me, "Lewis, we have to go. We've got to get on the bus." I apologized to those kids who didn't get an autograph and walked away. And as I did, several of the adults standing behind the kids started shouting at me, "Look at him, too big to sign autographs. Typical nigger." And so forth.

Coach stopped and looked at them. I could tell by his body language that he was thinking about confronting them. He'd look at the adults, then at the children. I knew that the fact that they'd said these things in front of those children is what pushed him to the edge of his Midwestern politeness. There was a darkness in his expression I hadn't seen before, and I was tempted to grab his arm and say, "It's okay, Coach. Just ignore them. Sometimes I startle people." But I didn't say or do anything. I was too surprised after all the time I'd spent signing autographs.

He finally wrestled his anger under control, glared at them with a laser beam of pure disgust that should have melted their faces. On the bus ride home, he walked back and slid in next to me. His face still looked troubled. I had already, if not forgotten the incident, shoved it back into the overflowing file cabinet of my mind with all the other similar incidents.

"Those people were wrong," he began. "You can't judge all people by the actions of a few." He paused, maybe looking for a poem, a quote, a story like he usually used to make his point. He couldn't find one. He pressed ahead anyway. "I know we have to have penitentiaries and police and laws, but most people are good. They're good."

Are they, Coach? I wanted to say. But I knew he believed that with all his heart, and so I wanted to believe it, too, for his sake. There was just too much evidence to the contrary. Still, even at my young age, I knew this talk wasn't about racism, it was him worrying about my soul. He didn't want me to become hardened and nasty, like some of the activists he saw on TV. He knew me as polite, respectful, good-natured Lewis who had a bright future if he didn't succumb to the dark side.

He returned to his seat. I hadn't needed another pep talk about the good hearts of white people. Yet, at the same time, I had needed a few kind words from someone who clearly cared about me beyond the number of points I could score. Just by coming back to check on me, he'd made the point that maybe most people really were good. Because of him, I hadn't altogether abandoned that hope.

It wasn't until years later that I found out that because of me he'd begun to question his own belief in the innate goodness of people. I was reading an interview with Coach and was surprised to come across these words: "I had no idea how tough it was for him at times. I learned more from Kareem about man's inhumanity to man than I ever learned anywhere else...I had never imagined that people could feel or talk like that." I felt a deep sadness after reading that, knowing my presence had caused him to doubt his fundamental beliefs.

But there was no doubting his own innate goodness. When Wilt Chamberlain was traded to the Lakers in 1968, he complained about his reputation of being "hard to handle." "I am not an animal, I'm a man," Wilt snapped. "You don't 'handle' a man." As soon as Coach read that, he contacted his publisher and told them that they had to change any new editions of his book, *Practical Modern Basketball*. The chapter previously titled "Handling Your Players" had to be changed to "Working with Your Players." When it came to racism, maybe he couldn't change the world, but he could change his world.

* * *

My development as a basketball player paralleled my evolution as a social activist. The more confident and successful I was on the court, the more confident I felt about expressing my political convictions. That personal progression reached its most controversial climax in 1968, when I refused to join the Olympic basketball team. This started a firestorm of criticism, racial epithets, and death threats that people still ask me about today.

I didn't reach that decision easily. I really, really wanted to join the team. It would be an exciting challenge to play against the best basketball players in the world as well as to be on the same team as the best college players in the country. Plus, the adventure of going to Mexico City and hanging with athletes from around the world appealed to the young man in me.

But the idea of going to Mexico to have fun seemed so selfish in light of the racial violence that was facing the country. The previous summer had seen two major riots, one in Newark that had lasted five days, and one in Detroit that had lasted eight days. And on April 4, 1968, Dr. Martin Luther King, Jr., had been assassinated. White America seemed ready to do anything necessary to stop the progress of civil rights, and I thought that going to Mexico would seem like I was either fleeing the issue or more interested in my career than in justice. I couldn't shake the feeling that if I did go and we won, I'd be bringing honor to the country that was denying our rights. It was the same feeling I'd had that last year playing for Coach Donahue after he'd called me a nigger.

I seemed to permanently reside in the exclusive neighborhood of Between a Rock and a Hard Place.

That same year *The Autobiography of Malcolm X* was published, posthumously since he'd been assassinated three years earlier. I didn't just read it, I devoured every chapter, every page, every word. His story couldn't have been more different than mine—street hustler and pimp who goes to prison, converts to Islam, emerges as an enlightened political leader—but I felt as if every insult he suffered and every insight he discovered were mine. He put into words what was in my heart; he clearly articulated what I had only vaguely expressed.

Malcolm was dead. Dr. King was dead.

Black leaders were an endangered species. That enraged me. There had been public accusations that the U.S. government, specifically J. Edgar Hoover and the FBI, were targeting black leaders in secret campaigns to discredit, humiliate, and publicly ruin them. White America dismissed this as black paranoia due to lack of proof, but black Americans knew it was true simply from observation. It wasn't until two years later that these suspicions were confirmed, when anti-war activists broke into an FBI office in Media, Pennsylvania, and found classified documents that detailed the FBI's active policy of intimidation against black leaders.

It was too difficult for me to get enthusiastic about representing a country that refused to represent me or others of my color. Another reason I chose not to participate was my intense dislike for the International Olympic Committee's president, Avery Brundage, who, during the 1936 Olympics in Berlin, benched two Jewish runners so as not to embarrass Adolph Hitler by having Jews win a gold medal. Not only was this against the Olympic rules, but information has since been revealed that Brundage's construction company was bidding for German contracts, which is why he was so eager to please Hitler. I couldn't bring myself to work under the supervision of someone like that. America was angry at me for not showing gratitude to the country that had given me so many opportunities. I was grateful, but I also thought it disingenuous to show appreciation unless all people had the same opportunities. Just because I had made it to a lifeboat didn't mean I could forget those who hadn't. Or not try to keep the next ship from sinking.

To their credit, no one at UCLA tried to talk me out of my decision. Coach Wooden respected my choice and never brought it up. The university issued a statement explaining that I had turned down the invitation because it conflicted with classes, but I openly discussed my decision with the press. Joe Garagiola interviewed me on the *Today* show in a contentious segment in which he proclaimed the usual motto of entitled white people: America, love it or leave it. I couldn't help but wonder what he would have said to the colonists who declared independence and fought to create their own country. Britain, love it or leave it.

I tried to make the point that true patriotism is about acknowledging problems and, rather than running away from them, joining together to fix them.

Although I missed the Olympics, Tommie Smith and John Carlos made international news and Olympic history when, during the medal ceremony for the men's 200-meter sprint, in which Smith received the gold medal and Carlos the bronze medal, they raised their gloved fists into the air in what was then known as the "Black Power salute." This was a gesture of acknowledgment of the racial injustice in America. The U.S. Olympic Committee suspended them. They returned home to angry criticism and death threats. At a time when black leaders were routinely slaughtered, death threats were taken seriously.

Although Coach Wooden didn't discuss my choice with me, I had the feeling that he disapproved, though not because of anything he said or did, even indirectly. I just knew that he was very patriotic. He had been a lieutenant in the navy during World War II. I couldn't imagine him endorsing my refusal to play in the Olympics and bring glory to the U.S.

I found out years later just how wrong I was.

A couple years ago I received a letter from a woman I had never met, a letter to her that Coach Wooden had written in response to a note she had sent to him complaining about my decision not to participate in the Olympics. Until I'd held it in my hands, I hadn't even known it existed. I opened the letter and began to read Coach's neat script:

> *Dear Mrs. Hough,*
>
> *The comments of this most unusual young man also disturbed me, but I have seen him hurt so much by the remarks of white people that I am probably more tolerant than most.*
>
> *I have heard remarks within his hearing such as "Hey, look at that big black freak," "Did you ever see such a big N----r?" and others of a similar nature that might tend to turn the head of a more mature person in normal times. I am truly afraid that he will never find any peace of mind regardless or not of whether he makes a million dollars. He may be able to afford material things, but they are a poor substitute for true peace of mind.*
>
> *You may not have seen or read about the later interview when he said that there were so many things wrong at present of the treatment of his race in this country that it was difficult for him to claim it as his own.*
>
> *Thank you for your interest,*
John Wooden

I read the letter again. Then again. *Oh, Coach, I* thought, *I wish I'd known how you felt.* If only to ease the burden you'd taken on to defend me. I thought back on my own arrogance at thinking I understood the man by reducing him to the kind of easy stereotype, the very thing that I'd been complaining about my whole life when it was done to me. He'd been too humble ever to say anything to me about the letter. Most people would have made a point of telling me how they'd come to my defense. But Coach Wooden didn't care about receiving credit. A good deed was its own reward. Seeking praise or gratitude would have negated the deed.

Coach Dale Brown once asked him why he didn't take some credit for the things he'd done or why he hadn't been more outspoken about the civil rights movement. Brown recalled, "He held up his thumb and index finger so closely together you barely could slide a piece of onionskin between them. 'That's why,' he said. I asked him what he meant and he explained, 'That's how much difference I would have made. So I tried to make a difference in other things.'"

I shook my head as I folded up the letter. Coach had been dead for several years and I would never get to thank him. Even then, at my age of sixty-seven, he was still teaching me about humility.

* * *

In 2008, I flew to Chicago to interview Coach Wooden for a documentary film I was producing on the Harlem

Rens, the greatest basketball team no one had ever heard of. I knew Coach had played against them in his youth and would have some good anecdotes for my movie. We had been friends for nearly fifty years, and I was pretty sure I knew everything about him, based on our years at UCLA and, later, the many lazy afternoons chatting in his cluttered den about everything from literature to religion to the men's Olympic basketball team going to Beijing. But that day Coach Wooden surprised me to the point that my mouth dropped open in shock. Then, before I could recover, he surprised me again.

I had rented a special room for filming interviews at the Marriott near the convention center. When Coach walked into the room I felt my body involuntarily straighten up just like any schoolboy whose favorite teacher approaches him. I was a sixty-year-old man and father of five children, and an international celebrity, yet the opinion of this elderly man shuffling into the room mattered more to me than anyone else's. I saw him as a second father, in some ways a more compassionate, hands-on father than my own had been.

"Hey, Coach," I said to him, "thanks for coming today. I really appreciate it."

"Anything for you," he said with a big smile that nudged my heart.

I tried not to show the pride I felt in the film. Pride would be unbecoming to Coach, who lived his life in strict modesty that bordered on monkishness. Though sometimes we players would poke fun at his Gandhi-like humility, secretly we all admired it and tried to emulate it. But it was like trying to become a vegan: It took a lot more discipline than most of us were capable of. Yet I wanted him to take at least a little pride in my accomplishments after I'd retired from basketball, because I felt that everything I had done since was a direct result of his influence. Even this film, an adaptation of *On the Shoulders of Giants*, a book I had written about the history of the Harlem Renaissance and its influence on America and me personally, was a result of his lessons. He had taught us that academics were more important than basketball and that personal integrity was more important than both.

In the years after basketball, I'd been on a crusade to bring more color to American history by writing history books that celebrated achievements by African-Americans that school textbooks conveniently overlooked. I'd written *Black Profiles in Courage*, about several influential blacks in American history; *Brothers in Arms*, about the all-black tank battalion in World War II; *On the Shoulders of Giants*; and I was in the process of doing research for a children's book, *What Color Is My World*, about overlooked black inventors who changed American culture. I wanted Coach to appreciate the fact that I had continued academics and writing, which as a former English teacher he had encouraged me to pursue.

"Where do you want me, Kareem?" he asked.

I showed him to his seat. Lights were aimed. The camera was focused. I started asking him questions. He responded just as I knew he would, with colorful and detailed stories about the Rens, describing them as the best team he had ever played against. The New York Renaissance, aka the Rens, were an all-black basketball team based in Harlem during the 1920s and 1930s, who won the first professional national championship tournament in 1939 against a white team.

We also discussed some of the great musicians, artists, and writers of the Harlem Renaissance.

"You know, Kareem, one of my favorite poets was Langston Hughes," he said.

"Really?" I said. He was one of my favorites, too. I'd first discovered him in high school—not in the classes where no black writers were ever mentioned, but at the Schomberg Center for Research in Black Culture in Harlem during the summer before my senior year of high school. I was mildly impressed that Coach knew him, but then he was one of the most famous black poets. If you were white and had to name one black poet, Langston Hughes was the go-to guy.

But to Coach, Langston Hughes wasn't just a name.

"'What happens to a dream deferred?'" he began reciting from memory. The poem was Langston Hughes's "Harlem." "'Does it dry up / like a raisin in the sun? / Or fester like a sore— / And then run? /

Does it stink like rotten meat? / Or crust and sugar over— / like a syrupy sweet? / Maybe it just sags / like a heavy load. / Or does it explode?'"

Surprise number one. Cue gaping mouth.

"Do you know why Mr. Hughes wrote such short lines?" he asked with a twinkle in his eye. He delighted in shocking me, especially at my age.

"Well, uh…" I stuttered.

"Because they used to pay him by the line. He figured by chopping the lines up he'd get paid more."

Old white man: 1. Middle-aged black man: 0.

He leaned back in his chair, no longer speaking for the camera but in full reminiscing mode. Just the two of us. Friend to friend. It was as if reciting that poem had reminded him of something he hadn't thought about in a long time. Maybe he was thinking about that old woman at the Bat Rack who had called me a nigger.

"You know, back in 1947 when I was in my first year coaching at Indiana State Teachers College, as it was known then. It's Indiana State University now. Anyway, we had just won the Indiana Intercollegiate Conference title and the National Association of Intercollegiate Athletics invited us to play in the National Basketball Tournament in Kansas City. It was a pretty big deal to the team and the school."

"Not to mention a first-time coach," I added.

He smiled impishly. "There was that." Then his face tightened a little, his mouth shifting into a slight frown. "But they had one condition. I couldn't bring Clarence Walker because he was black."

Second surprise. I hadn't heard this story before. I knew what I hoped he'd told them, but this wasn't a movie. He had been a first-time coach with a career to think of. A family to think of.

"I shouldn't have been surprised, I guess," he said. "But to tell the truth, I'm always surprised when people act poorly for no good reason. Lord knows Clarence had been through enough."

I didn't say anything. Coach was pulling more memories from storage. I was fascinated.

"Sometimes when the team was on the road, restaurants refused to serve him or hotels wouldn't let him stay there with the rest of the team."

"What did you do?" I asked.

That was the quintessential question in these situations, wasn't it? Not how did it make you feel, but what did you do about it? Maybe he thought my question was an accusation, arising from what had happened at the Bat Rack. I didn't mean it to be, so I backtracked. "I mean, what could you do?"

"I usually found other accommodations for him." He took a deep breath. "But one afternoon we stopped in a restaurant. The team took up four tables. After most of the boys had ordered, the waitress informed me that she wouldn't serve Clarence." He looked at me with steady eyes and smiled. "I told her that was unacceptable. She serves him or we all leave. She was pretty upset, probably calculating how much tip money she would be losing. She told me I couldn't do that. 'Watch us,' I said, and we all got up and walked out."

Always a team player, Coach, I thought fondly. "What did you do about the National Tournament's ultimatum?"

"Same thing I did at the restaurant. Told them we all play or none of us play." There was no bravado or pride in his voice. It was as if he were telling me what he'd had for lunch. "We all won the championship together, and we were going to play together or not at all. Their answer was not at all."

This had happened sixty years ago, and I was getting angry just hearing about it.

"The next year we won again, and the NAIB changed its policy so we played. We lost in the finals to Louisville. Only championship game I ever lost."

"What happened to Clarence Walker?"

"First African-American to play in a postseason intercollegiate basketball tournament."

I couldn't have been more surprised. Coach had been an early pioneer of civil rights, risking his own career, and he'd never told me about it. Any other coach would have used that as a way to gain my loyalty and respect. But Coach wanted to earn those on the court. What made Coach's stance all the more admirable, I found out later, was that Clarence Walker wasn't even a starter. The team could have done just fine without him. Except that, in Coach's mind, they would no longer have been a team. And that would have been the biggest sin.

I looked at the shrunken ninety-eight-year-old man sitting there with thick glasses and large jug ears and felt a tenderness for him that I had taken for granted. I had modeled myself after him in so many ways, and I was still learning how deep his influence ran. I realized that all my writings about black history, politics, and pop culture had one theme: making the playing field even so everyone has the same opportunities. Or, as Coach might say, "No one eats unless we all eat."

Chapter 4

What Would Wooden Do

Religion, Politics, and Keeping the Faith

"You can do more good by being good than any other way."

—*John Wooden*

From all outward appearances, you'd think Coach Wooden was an Orville Redenbacher look-alike who embodied conservative Midwestern values and preached unbendable Christian morals. But you'd be very, very wrong. Coach was a much more complex person than any convenient stereotype, a characteristic we both shared. The difference was that I battled my racial stereotype in a public forum of hostility, while he fought his quietly through his behind-the-scenes deeds that people rarely heard about. I was passionate about changing white America's perception of black people so they could see us as their equals, deserving our Constitutional rights; he didn't care about how people saw him, he cared about doing the right thing. Nowhere was his complexity more evident, and his views more surprising, than in our interaction over the years regarding politics and religion. These twin topics of doom have destroyed more friendships and family dinners than anything else, yet they brought us closer together, even though we often disagreed.

At no time in American history were the subjects of religion and politics more contentious or did they inspire more animosity than during my years at UCLA and a few years after. Between the rise of the civil rights movement in 1964 and the fall of Saigon in 1975, the United States was a battleground of riots, marches, and protests. It started with blacks seeking voting rights, but soon grew to include college students and veterans protesting the Vietnam War, and women seeking liberation from sexual, social, and political repression. The Vietnam War (1955–1975) brought the protesting factions of blacks, anti-war demonstrators, and advocates for women's liberation together to seek civil rights for all. The resulting violence and turmoil in the streets and on campuses frightened the white male conservative establishment, who were anxious to restore order by turning back the clock to the 1950s, when women and blacks were treated as children, and children did as they were told. The deadly consequences of this cultural and generational clash resulted in the National Guard opening fire at a Kent State University protest rally in 1970, killing four students. After that, there was no going back.

In the middle of the greatest cultural revolution in American history, I played basketball.

And Coach Wooden taught basketball.

But what was happening around us couldn't be ignored—especially because I was an enthusiastic part of it and he wasn't. Inevitably, we clashed.

* * *

The most controversial political figure in America during this time was heavyweight boxing champion Muhammad Ali. Americans were passionately divided about how they felt about Ali. You loved him or you hated him. There was no in-between. On one side were the mainstream, Main Street, middle-class whites, who condemned Ali for being ungrateful, a traitor, and a coward. On the other side were the New Order liberals, people of color, poor people, and other marginalized Americans shaking their fists in frustration, who admired Ali for his courage, outspokenness, and personal sacrifice.

On one side was Coach Wooden quoting Kipling: "If you can wait and not be tired by waiting."

On the other side was me quoting Malcolm X: "If you want something, you had better make some noise."

I first met Muhammad Ali in 1966 when I was a freshman. I was walking along Hollywood Boulevard with two school buddies when we saw him half a block ahead of us, doing sleight-of-hand magic tricks for fans who came up to him. He was one of the most famous athletes in the world—some say the greatest boxer who ever lived—and he was doing card tricks for strangers he could just as easily have dismissed with a quick autograph. The fans giggled with delight as they hurried away, and I couldn't help but admire his way with people. To him, fans weren't a burden, they were a blessing. And he made sure they knew it.

I filed that away for future reference, when the day came and fans would flock to me.

Because I was such a big fan of his, I overcame my shyness and approached him. He made no sign that he knew who I was. He was friendly and charming, just as he had been with the other fans. No more, no less. And then he moved on down the street with his small entourage, happy and cheerful, like a man with no worries. A year later he would be stripped of his championship title after announcing he would not submit to being drafted into the army. "I ain't got no quarrel with them Viet Cong," he said by way of explanation. "They never called me nigger." He claimed exemption on religious grounds as a Muslim: "My conscience won't let me go shoot my brother, or some darker people."

Ali had been an idol of mine since I was thirteen, back when he was still known as Cassius Clay. He had won a gold medal as a light heavyweight boxer in the 1960 Olympics. His skill, speed, and grace had inspired me to push myself even harder as an athlete. My admiration for him only grew over the next few years as he proved to be the most outspoken, irrepressible black athlete the country had ever seen. At that time, successful black entertainers and athletes who had been invited to sit at the table of power with whites were expected to be humble and grateful, but most of all quiet. But that wasn't Ali.

He'd risen to fame by bragging about his skills and brashly predicting in which round he would knock out his opponent. Many whites were so angered by this upstart black boy that they paid good money to see him put back into his place. That had been Ali's brilliant plan all along. It made him millions. He could have allowed himself to be drafted, knowing that the army wouldn't have put him in harm's way. They would have used him for recruiting. His life could have gone on as before. But for all his clowning and braying and performing, he was at heart a deeply moral man who placed conscience over commerce.

His public stance cost him everything. Not only was he stripped of his title and banned from boxing for three years, but he was fined $10,000, arrested, and threatened with a long prison sentence. In 1971, the U.S. Supreme Court overturned his conviction 8–0, but the damage had already been done. He had been removed from boxing during three years at the peak of his physical condition.

I met Ali again in my freshman year at a lavish party attended by many college and professional athletes. My shyness sent me wandering off by myself, eventually settling in at the drum kit the musicians had abandoned while on break. I had a nice little beat going when Ali suddenly slid onto a stool next to me and started strumming the guitar. After that night, Ali, who was only five years older, became a big brother figure to me.

A few months later, football great Jim Brown, who was by that time a Hollywood actor, invited me to join a group of black athletes and activists in Cleveland to discuss Ali's refusal to be drafted. I was only a sophomore at UCLA and, at twenty, the youngest person at what would become known as the Cleveland Summit. The meeting was to determine whether or not we would publicly support Ali in his refusal to be drafted. This was by no means a rubber-stamp committee. Several of the participants had been in the military. Brown himself had belonged to the Army ROTC and graduated from Syracuse University as a second lieutenant. Attorney Carl Stokes, who in a few months would become the mayor of Cleveland, making him the first black mayor of a major U.S. city, had served in World War II, just like Coach Wooden.

The summit was not even supposed to happen. It had started as a simple phone call to Brown from Ali's manager, Herbert Muhammad. Muhammad wanted Brown to help convince Ali to drop his refusal to be drafted to avoid the severe loss of income that could wipe Ali out financially, not to mention the public outcry. Muhammad was torn between his religious convictions, which were the same as Ali's, and his desire to protect his friend from ruin. To Muhammad, Brown seemed like a good choice to persuade Ali because he had been an outspoken activist for years, so Ali would listen. But Brown also was a partner in the company that promoted Ali's fights, so he had a financial stake in having Ali fighting.

Nevertheless Brown took his role seriously. He invited me and the rest of the summit members to sit as a jury in assessing Ali's sincerity and commitment. Every athlete responded by immediately agreeing to come at his own expense. I was excited to finally be part of the political movement in a more direct and active way, doing something important rather than just complaining. I also wanted to help Ali if I could, because he made me feel proud to be African-American.

On June 4, 1967, we gathered in the offices of the Negro Industrial Economic Union (NIEU), which soon became the Black Economic Union (BEU). Brown was the co-developer of the BEU, and I volunteered at the BEU Los Angeles chapter. Despite our admiration for Ali, we grilled him for hours. Many in the group had come with their minds already made up to persuade Ali to accept his military service. The discussions became pretty heated as questions and answers were fired back and forth. Pretty soon, though, we all realized

Ali was not going to change his mind. For two hours he lectured us on Islam, black pride, and his religious conviction that the Vietnam War was wrong.

We were all well aware that in the early days of the Vietnam War, kids who could afford to go to college were exempted from the draft, which left poor kids, many of them black, forced to go fight. It was a war against people of color fought by people of color for a country who denied them their basic civil rights. But this wasn't just about the politics; it was about Ali's understanding what the consequences of his actions would be, for him as well as the Nation of Islam. In the end, he convinced us, and we decided to support him. Bill Russell summed it up for all of us: "I envy Muhammad Ali . . . He has something I have never been able to attain and something very few people possess. He has absolute and sincere faith. I'm not worried about Muhammad Ali. He is better equipped than anyone I know to withstand the trials in store for him. What I'm worried about is the rest of us."

We did our best at that Cleveland Summit to support Ali's legal fight and to publicize the injustice of the draft, but we knew how powerless we were against those promoting the war. In January of 2017, fifty years after the summit, Jim Brown and I joined several other athletes and activists for a "Words to Action" symposium at San Jose State University's Institute for the Study of Sport, Society, and Social Change.

Being at that summit and hearing Ali's articulate defense of his moral beliefs and his willingness to suffer for them reinvigorated my commitment to become even more politically involved. That feeling of wanting to be part of a movement to ensure justice and opportunities for all Americans hasn't left me since.

Coach Wooden, however, was not a fan of Muhammad Ali.

After the bombing of Pearl Harbor, John Wooden left his wife, son, and daughter, and his career as a high school English teacher, coach, and professional basketball player to join the navy. He served as a physical education instructor for four years during World War II. When a sudden attack of appendicitis prevented Lieutenant Wooden from shipping out with his buddies for the South Pacific on the U.S.S. *Franklin*, he was quickly replaced by his friend and fraternity brother, Purdue quarterback Freddie Stalcup. Shortly thereafter, the *Franklin* was attacked by a Japanese kamikaze plane that crashed into the ship, killing Stalcup. The loss of his friend, as well as the knowledge that it could have been him who died, made Coach cherish the sacrifices of soldiers. It also made him less tolerant of those who shirked their military duty.

While I was at UCLA, Coach and I never had an extended conversation about Ali, but he would drop comments critical of Ali now and then. He knew Ali and I were friends, so his remarks were always in passing, as if he was trying to subliminally influence me, like a clumsy hypnotist. "First he's Cassius Clay, then he's Muhammad Ali. Hmph." "It's a privilege, not an obligation, to fight for your country." "Can't he see he's hurting the country?" Like that.

I ignored these comments. I felt like the child of divorced parents who had to listen to one beloved parent complain about the other beloved parent. I respected and admired both of them, and I wanted to maintain my relationship with both. Despite my growing political activism, I still loved basketball. It was an island of refuge for me. I knew the rules, I had the skills, and the outcome was always clean and pure. With politics, there never seemed to be a resolution, just more obstacles.

Ali was an irritant between us, but not a relationship breaker. I respected Coach's position as a veteran, but I knew Ali was on the right path, a path that Coach couldn't understand. He was too loyal to old ideas to accept any new ideas easily. To me, he was like the U.S. Constitution: the original had some flaws (like not providing rights for women and permitting slavery), but it also had provisions to evolve with the times, to grow in order to fulfill the spirit of equality that defined the document. Coach was never static in his beliefs, but evolved over the years as he read more and observed more. By 2009, he told an interviewer that he would describe himself politically as a liberal Democrat who had voted for some Republican presidential candidates.

Whatever his beliefs when I played for him, he never openly judged my beliefs. In April of 1968, just after Dr. King had been assassinated, I joined in a campus demonstration in support of Dr. King's political agenda. This was as laid-back as a protest rally could get: a bunch of students standing around Bruin Walk carrying signs for an hour. We were so polite and unaggressive we could have been gathering for a tie-dye demonstration. Still, we enraged some people, who felt compelled to ask me what I was doing. "You're going to play in the NBA some day and make millions! Why aren't you more grateful? This country gave you everything! You're gonna be richer than most white people!" I tried to be patient and explain that my success had nothing to do with the issues, but they didn't want to hear it.

Coach Wooden knew all about my participation at the protest, but he never said a word to me. No dirty looks. No biting comments in passing. He acted as if he didn't know about it, which I chose to take as approval.

The closest he ever came to admitting directly to me that my anti-war activities were valid was years later when we were having lunch in Westwood. He was telling me about an English class he'd taught once and how hard it was to get the students to appreciate

Shakespeare. "To them, Shakespeare's plays were tales 'told by an idiot, full of sound and fury, signifying nothing.'"

"Is that from *Fiddler on the Roof*?" I joked.

"*Macbeth*," he said, taking a bite of his grilled cheese sandwich.

"How do you remember all those quotes?"

"Years of teaching English, Kareem. I couldn't forget it if I tried."

"You should go on *Jeopardy*. You'd make a fortune."

He didn't answer. Making money had never been a big motivation for him to do anything. He did things out of love or duty, never money.

"You know what I never understood?" I said. "Why you quit teaching English. You clearly have a passion for literature."

His eyes brightened, and I knew I'd jogged a happy memory. "I had a realization when I was in the navy. While I was away, I had been getting all these letters from my basketball players, but hardly any from my English students. I understood right then that I'd had a greater impact on my players than on my students. Something about sports, the competitiveness, the practices, that brings you closer together."

"Sweat binds more than glue," I said.

He laughed. "I may use that."

Then he was quiet a moment. "But sometimes I miss the classroom, the stories, the plays, the poems." He looked at me as if trying to communicate something without using words. "You know Thomas Hardy?"

"I read *Return of the Native* in sophomore English. That's pretty much the extent of my knowledge."

He took a sip of ice water, then recited: "'They throw in Drummer Hodge, to rest / Uncoffined—just as found: / His landmark is a kopje-crest / That breaks the veldt around: / And foreign constellations west / Each night above his mound.'"

I had no idea what he was talking about. I didn't want to say that, in case this was an age thing. I resisted the urge to say, "Hardy har har."

"It's about a young British soldier, no more than fifteen, during the Boer War in South Africa. He's never been away from home before, and he's killed. He gets thrown into an open hole without a coffin. A kopje is a hill, which tells us he has nothing to mark his grave. For the rest of eternity, this child will lie under unfamiliar stars far from home."

I said nothing. Just listened.

"Thing is, that poem about a war in the late 1800s is just as pertinent today as it was then. It never stops, Kareem. It never stops."

Was he telling me I was right about protesting the Vietnam War, or was he just fed up with war in general?

I got a clue in 2007 when he returned from Louisville, Kentucky, where he had gone as part of his duties helping to run the McDonald's High School

All-American program. While there, he visited the Louisville bat factory that turned out the famous Louisville Slugger, and the Muhammad Ali Center. Given his earlier disapproval of Ali, I was surprised that, at ninety-seven, he had gone to the effort. I knew he had been a boxing coach in the navy while stationed in Iowa. The days were too hot for basketball, so they assigned him to teach the cadets boxing. But this trip seemed to be motivated by more than love of the sport.

The next time Coach and I got together, he was brimming with questions about Ali. What was he like? How bad was his Parkinson's? Did I see him at all? Ali used to come to some of my games when I was with the Lakers, and I would go to some of his boxing matches. We still stayed in touch, but his health kept him from traveling much.

Coach was so excited to be talking about Ali that I was happy to dredge up a story I remembered from a time he'd come to see me play at the Forum in 1980, a few weeks before he was to fight his old sparring partner, Larry Holmes. "When he walked into the locker room, I just stared," I told Coach. "I was shocked to see him in such poor shape. He had a gut, and his face was all puffed out. I told him right then that he needed to quit. We all wanted him to quit. But, you know, he wouldn't listen. He just thought he was going to go on forever."

"Don't we all," he answered with a grin. "Don't we all."

"He completely ignored me and asked how much I weighed. When I told him two hundred fifty pounds, he laughed and said, 'Hey, me, too.'"

"That was too much weight for him to carry," Coach said. "It took away from his quickness."

"That's what I told him," I said. "He just laughed as if there was nothing he couldn't handle. But you could see he had started taking shortcuts. He was taking diuretics to lose the water weight."

"That's not good. Causes dehydration, reduces potassium in the blood; you can get headaches and muscle cramps. I've seen it before."

"It's just like you always told us, Coach, if you want to be your best, you can't take shortcuts. I still live by that."

He smiled, pleased that I remembered his lessons.

"See," I said, "I can quote great people, too."

"Goodness, Kareem," he protested softly, turning his head so I couldn't see his face.

* * *

During my time at UCLA, religion was going through some massive changes around the country. The hypocrisy of the Vietnam War and the backlash against blacks in the civil rights movement and women in the women's liberation movement left a lot of the youth feeling disillusioned about those in charge. We had pulled back the curtain to reveal that the wizard was nothing more than self-serving businesspeople and their lackey politicians profiting from the war, profiting from slum properties, and profiting from paying women less. Because many religions were backing the status quo, they lost credibility, and people started to explore alternative faiths and belief systems. Communes were on the rise, Scientology was growing, human potential movements like est were popular. People were paying thousands of dollars to sit in a room and not be allowed to pee, or attend a retreat to hit each other with padded clubs.

Those shaking their heads at these alternatives missed the point. People had lost faith in the goodness of their country, their religion, their society. They were desperate to have faith in something.

I had been raised a Catholic, attended Catholic schools, went to mass almost every Sunday until I moved out of my parents' home to attend UCLA. My relationship with Catholicism had always been shaky. The Catholic school curriculum had ignored any black people in history who had done anything heroic, remarkable, or innovative. I had discovered hundreds of artists, writers, scientists, political leaders, soldiers, and inventors who had profoundly influenced the history of America, yet they were left out of the history books. Worse, the white people who were bombing churches and killing little girls, who were shooting unarmed black boys, who were beating black protestors with clubs loudly declared they were proud Christians. The Ku Klux Klan were proud Christians.

I felt no allegiance to a religion that had so many evil followers. Yes, I was also aware that the Reverend Dr. Martin Luther King, Jr., was also a proud Christian, as were many of the civil rights leaders. Coach Wooden was a devout Christian. The civil rights movement was supported by many brave white Christians who marched side by side with blacks. When the KKK attacked, they often delivered even worse beatings to the whites, whom they considered to be race traitors. I didn't condemn the religion, but I definitely felt removed from it.

Part of my dilemma was that I came to realize that the Lew Alcindor everyone was cheering wasn't really the person they wanted me to be. They wanted me to be the clean-cut example of racial equality, the poster boy for how anybody from any background, regardless of race, religion, or economic standing, could become an American Success Story. To them, I was the living proof that racism was a mythological beast like the Minotaur. But I knew that was a fantasy contrived to make people feel good so they could ignore the terrors of living in poverty with little chance of breaking out.

I couldn't help but wonder if that wasn't how Coach Wooden saw me, too. As much as I appreciated all he had done for me, I couldn't be someone I wasn't, even for him. If anything, I owed my confidence to express myself to the training that he'd given me. The better a player he made me, the more self-assured I was in pushing myself intellectually. And the better player I became, the more we won; the more we won, the more famous I became, which gave me a platform to express my opinions, especially about racial inequality.

I started reading about Islam as a freshman, both in books about religion and in *The Autobiography of Malcolm X*. When solo study wasn't enough, I found a teacher in Hamaas Abdul Khaalis in 1968. My father recommended him after Hamaas warned my father about the perils of joining the Black Muslims. During my years playing with the Milwaukee Bucks, Hamaas taught me his version of Islam, which I embraced enthusiastically. Then in 1971, when I was twenty-four, I converted to Islam and became Kareem Abdul-Jabbar ("the noble one, servant of the Almighty").

The backlash was instant and brutal. Fans acted as if I had thrown flaming bags of poop at their churches while urinating on the American flag. I tried to explain that I wasn't so much rejecting Christianity as I was embracing a religion that was more in keeping with my cultural background (20–30 percent of slaves brought from Africa were Muslims). Fans also thought I had joined the Nation of Islam, an American Islamic movement founded in Detroit in 1930, which Muhammad Ali belonged to. Although I had been greatly influenced by Nation of Islam member Malcolm X, I chose not to join because I wanted to focus more on the spiritual rather than political aspects. Eventually, Malcolm rejected the group, right before three of its members assassinated him.

The adoption of a new name reflected my rejection of all things in my life that related to the enslavement of my family and people. Alcindor was the name of a French planter in Trinidad who owned my ancestors. My ancestors were Yoruba people, from present-day Nigeria or Benin. Keeping the name of my family's slave master seemed to dishonor them. His name felt like a branded scar of shame.

My devotion to Islam was absolute. I even agreed to marry a woman that Hamaas had suggested for me, despite my strong feelings for another woman. Ever the team player, I did as "Coach" Hamaas recommended. I also followed his advice not to invite my parents to the wedding, a mistake that took me more than decade to rectify. Although I had my doubts about some of Hamaas's instruction, I rationalized them away because of the great spiritual fulfillment I was experiencing.

But my independent spirit finally emerged. Not content to receive all my religious knowledge from one man, I pursued my own studies. I soon found that I disagreed with some of Hamaas's teachings about the Qur'an and we parted. In 1973, I traveled to Libya and Saudi Arabia to learn enough Arabic to study the Qur'an on my own. I emerged from this quest with my beliefs clarified and my faith renewed.

From that year to this, I have never wavered nor regretted my decision to convert to Islam. When I look back now, I wish I could have done it in a more private way, without all the publicity and fuss that followed. But at the time, I was adding my voice to the civil rights movement by denouncing the legacy of slavery and the religious institutions that had supported it. That made it more political than I had intended and distracted from what was, for me, a much more personal journey.

* * *

My religious conversion was never an issue for Coach Wooden. The first time he had to confront it directly was at the NCAA semifinals in 1968. After the game, I did something I had never done before: I put on a brightly colored red, orange, and yellow African robe, which I referred to as my "dignity robe." My joy that night was more powerful than my reticence. It wasn't meant to be a challenge to anyone; it simply was my statement that I was finding my roots.

As I walked across the locker room floor, my dashiki swishing just below my knees, I felt just a bit rebellious and defiant—like I was daring anyone to say something. Coach Wooden, who had been talking with a reporter, turned at the sound and saw me in all my bright peacock finery. He hesitated while he took it all in, then smiled broadly like a father watching his son in a school play. I felt relieved by his smile and continued out of the room with just a bit more bounce in my step.

I hadn't spoken about my religious conversion with anyone on the team. I wasn't being mysterious or secretive, I just didn't know how to bring it up. "Hey, fellas, let's go out tonight and crush those jackasses. And by the way, I'm now a Muslim. Go Bruins!"

Even though no one on the team brought it up to me or commented on it, they all knew. But they acted as if they didn't. It was as if I had announced a terminal disease and they didn't want to distress me by talking about it. Coach Wooden wouldn't say anything because he would have thought it was none of his business. To him, each person had to go on his or her own spiritual journey. He was probably happy that at least I was on a spiritual journey, because that meant I cared about doing the right thing.

Then came the night when it finally was brought in the open in front of the whole team, including Coach Wooden. That simple bus ride, like so many we had taken before, became one of the most memorable nights of my life, a night we would all talk about for many years to come. Bill Sweek later described it as "an iconic moment in my life and our team's life; a spiritual experience I have never forgotten." Kenny Heitz also remembered that night as special: "It's the most memorable moment of the years I spent at UCLA. It was a bunch of guys really talking, no barriers. It was just deeply special."

It was early December, 1968. We had just beaten thirteenth-ranked Ohio State in Columbus and were on our way to South Bend to play fifth-ranked Notre Dame. It was late at night, we were tired, and the bus was quiet. We weren't singing, snapping jock straps, or drawing mustaches on sleeping teammates. For us, it was strictly a business trip. Some people were nodding off or just staring out the window at the dark fields; others were engaged in quiet discussions. I was sitting near sophomore Steve Patterson, my backup at center.

There were several different religions represented on our team that year: five or six Christians, several of them evangelicals; two Jews; and me, the only Muslim. Steve Patterson was a born-again Christian, who was not reticent about sharing his beliefs. He thought that everyone should be a Christian if they had any hope of saving their souls and not going to hell. He wasn't being arrogant, but seemed to be speaking from a heartfelt concern about the eternal lives of his teammates. He couldn't bear to think of them suffering in hell. It was clear that he had no clue about my recent conversion. I was only half listening as he loudly proclaimed his beliefs. I'd been hearing this stuff all my life in Catholic school after Catholic school.

But finally he went a little too far for me when he said, "You know, Christ died for all men. Christ is the only salvation if you don't want to go to hell."

"Wait a second, Steve," I interrupted. "What about all those people around the world who never heard of Christ? Aren't they going to be saved?"

Steve shook his head. "No, I don't think so."

"Thanks a lot, Steve," John Ecker snorted.

"Let me get this straight," I said to Steve. "Some little toddler in India dies of cholera, and she goes straight to hell?"

He hesitated. "Probably purgatory."

"Why purgatory? She's just a child. She didn't do anything wrong."

"We're all born in sin, Lew," he replied.

"But she's not guilty of anything."

"We're all guilty. Because of Eve. Read your Bible, man."

"I've read it, Steve. And it doesn't make a whole lot of sense."

"It does if you *really* read it."

"I *really* read it. Which is how I know that purgatory is never mentioned in the Bible. The word isn't even used as a noun until the twelfth century."

It was the same discussion that was probably happening in a hundred dorm rooms across the country, with students just as earnest and just as sure they were in the right.

As our voices rose, other teammates turned to listen. Maybe they were hoping for a fistfight, or maybe they were just interested in the discussion. At the front of the bus I could see the back of Coach Wooden's head bent over whatever Western novel he was reading. Either he didn't hear us or he didn't want to get involved. Things could have gone badly: two highly competitive guys who each felt they had the inside lane to enlightenment. But, whatever our petty disagreement, Steve was a truly decent person who wanted to be good and do the right thing. He was active in Campus Crusade for Christ and had even started a ministry on campus, the Jesus Christ Light and Power House, which housed and served not just Christians but students of all faiths. He didn't just talk the talk, he walked the walk, and I respected him for that.

Instead of escalating into a shouting match, Steve and I both switched gears and started listening to the other guy. We stopped trying to be right and just tried to get to better know each other's beliefs. Other players, who were sitting spread out throughout the bus, heard our voices and began moving closer to us. Eventually almost the entire team was gathered in the middle of the bus, leaning over the seats to participate. A few of them began voicing their own opinions. No one was attempting to simply defend their beliefs; instead everyone was listening and asking questions. We all opened up that night, as we drove through the dark Indiana countryside, with a trusting intimacy that we had never experienced before. Some talked about how they questioned their own faith, others how they had lost their faith. Some spoke about how leaving home brought them closer to their faith. Never had we been closer to each other as individuals, never had we been closer as a team. Never would we be this close again.

Which is why I suddenly felt the compulsion to say, "For those who haven't heard, I've converted to Orthodox Islam."

There was the kind of silence you might hear in deep outer space.

I braced myself for the onslaught. Now that I'd opened Pandora's box, I expected the usual venom to follow. But it didn't. Some already knew. Those who didn't know were only mildly surprised. They knew I was studying religion, philosophy, and politics. They could see the books I always had with me on the bus trips or in the locker room: Eldridge Cleaver's *Soul on Ice*, William Barrett's *Irrational Man: A Study in Existential Philosophy*, and, of course, *The Autobiography of Malcolm X*. Instead of judging me, they expressed a lively curiosity about the process that led me to make that decision and about what it meant to be a Muslim.

"What's the difference between Black Muslim and, uh, regular Muslim?"

"Why did Muslims kill Malcolm X if he was also a Muslim?"

"Who the heck is Malcolm X?" Bill Sweek asked.

"You ever read a newspaper, Bill?" Kenny Heitz said.

Laughter.

"Only to make sure they spell my name right," Bill responded.

More laughter.

Coach Wooden, hearing that we were laughing instead of shouting, made his way back and joined us, but only to ask the occasional question, not to moderate or direct the conversation. I glanced over at him a few times to see if I could gauge his reaction about my announcement, but all I saw was a wide smile of joy, not at me, but at the team. His boys weren't just basketball players, they were the mature, respectful gentlemen he wanted us to be. For him, that was more important than any championship.

Coach was also worried about our afterlife. But to him that meant life after basketball. To him, basketball was a teaching tool to prepare us to live rich, fulfilling lives as fathers, husbands, and community members. For a couple hours that night in December, he knew he didn't have to worry about our afterlife.

* * *

Coach Wooden was a devout Christian who once said, "If I were ever prosecuted for my religion, I truly hope there would be enough evidence to convict me." But he was also a man who admired simplicity. Rather than going around quoting the Bible, he relied on a card his father had given him and his brothers when they graduated from elementary school. On one side was a verse by the Reverend Henry Van Dyke, who was famous for his many poems and short stories:

> *Four things a man must learn to do*
> *If he would make his life more true:*
> *To think without confusion clearly,*
> *To love his fellow-man sincerely,*
> *To act from honest motives purely,*
> *To trust in God and Heaven securely.*

On the other side of the card was a list titled, "Seven Things to Do":

1. Be true to yourself.
2. Make each day your masterpiece.
3. Help others.
4. Drink deeply from good books, especially the Bible.
5. Make friendship a fine art.

6. Build a shelter against a rainy day.
7. Pray for guidance and give thanks for your blessings every day.

Coach renamed the list his "Seven Point Creed" and continued to live by it, as well as teach it to others.

Over the course of our friendship, I saw him demonstrate his commitment to these teachings on a daily basis. But the last one was especially pertinent on Thanksgiving of my sophomore year when he invited me to his daughter's house for a traditional dinner.

I was too broke to go home to New York, so a couple friends of mine, Ray and Julian, came down to visit me. We had grown up together in New York, but they were now playing basketball at a junior college in Wyoming. Coach was kind enough to invite them to come to dinner with me. The day was a little cool for southern California because it had just rained for a few days before. We drove to Coach's daughter's house in the San Fernando Valley, getting lost a couple times on the way and having to call the house for directions. We showed up late, but no one minded. It was that kind of family. That kind of day.

The house was modest. Nan, his daughter, welcomed us with enthusiasm as if we were cousins she hadn't seen in ages. Coach's son, James, was also there, and just as warm and hospitable. Nan's little children were playing on the living room floor with the TV showing the Macy's Thanksgiving Day Parade. I felt a twinge of homesickness when I saw that because my father used to take me to watch the parade. Because of that, I continued to watch it every year far into adulthood.

I carried the children around on my back, which delighted them to no end. They had never been lifted that high in the air before. "Look, Mommy, I'm flying," they squealed as I zoomed them around the room.

Coach was more relaxed than I'd ever seen him. Today he was just Grandpa and Dad and Friend. Not Coach. He had to adjust himself in the easy chair every few minutes because of his bad back. In the navy he'd gotten knocked into a steel post during a game of basketball, and it had done serious injury to his spine, requiring several surgeries. That was why he walked a little hunched over, which became more pronounced as he got older.

Dinner was traditional as advertised. Turkey, gravy, mashed potatoes, stuffing. If it was a dish featured in a Hallmark card for Thanksgiving, it was on this table. And I was glad for it.

Dinner conversation was light. Nan poked fun at Coach's superstitious rituals. I knew about his pregame habit of pulling up his socks, spitting on the floor, rubbing the spit with his shoe, rubbing his hands, and patting his assistant on the leg.

"Did you know about the hairpins?" Nan asked.

If Coach was embarrassed, he didn't show it. He seemed pleased by the attention of his family.

"No," I said. "Hairpins?"

"Every time he finds a hairpin, he has to stick it into the nearest piece of wood. Tree, table, porch, doesn't matter."

"I read that the St. Louis Cardinals used to do that," Coach said as if that were the most reasonable explanation in the world.

"Sometimes on game day," Nell chimed in, "I deliberately leave a hairpin lying around just so he can do that."

They described how whenever he would find a coin on the ground, he would stick it in his left shoe and walk around with it all day.

And so on for over an hour. I hadn't felt so at home, so comfortable just sitting around with people, in the two years since I'd left home.

After dinner, Coach and I sat in the living room. Julian and Ray were taking their turn playing with the kids. James, Nell, and Nan were in the kitchen, having refused our offer of help cleaning up.

"Give thanks for your blessings every day," he said. It was half of number seven of the list his father had given him. "You know why I give thanks every day and not just Thanksgiving?"

"Your family?" I guessed. It seemed to be the kind of sappy thing older people always said.

He squirmed in his chair again. "You know about how I missed my ship during the war because I was ill. How my college friend who took my place died?"

I nodded. I'd heard about it somewhere.

"I also heard you used to cut practice short on Tuesday nights so you could hurry home to watch a TV show."

He nodded. "Yup. *The Life and Legend of Wyatt Earp*. That was before your time."

"Not really. I used to watch that show all the time."

"Hugh O'Brian played Wyatt Earp. Did you know he was in the Marines in World War II? At seventeen, he was their youngest drill instructor ever."

Where does he come up with this stuff? I wondered. "You still love the Westerns, though. You're always reading them on the bus."

He smiled at me. "You know why I like Westerns, Lewis?"

"Lots of action?" That's why I liked them.

"That doesn't hurt. But mostly I like them because there's a clear good guy and a clear bad guy. The good guy knows what the right thing to do is if he wants to defeat the bad guy." His smile broadened. "And he always does the right thing."

"That's not realistic," I said, my political ire seeping in. "It's not that kind of world."

"No, it's not," he said. "But it could be. It could be."

That was one of the most valuable lessons I learned from Coach, and he taught it to me over and over again. It wasn't enough to just focus on how bad things were; we also needed to have a dream of what could be. And we had to have faith in ourselves that we could make that dream come true. Or, as he often said, quoting poet Robert Browning, "A man's reach should exceed his grasp, / Or what's a heaven for?"

Chapter 5

We've Got Trouble, Right Here in Pauley Pavilion

Getting Lost on Wooden Way

"Things work out best for the people who make the best of the way things work out."
—*John Wooden*

At the end of one of Coach Wooden's favorite Western movies, *The Man Who Shot Liberty Valance*, a reporter is asked whether he'll print the true story that contradicts the popular legend of how the villain Liberty Valance was shot. In doing so, he would destroy a beloved story of a heroic shootout. The reporter replies wryly, "This is the West, sir. When the legend becomes fact, print the legend."

While I recognize that much of my experience with Coach adds to his legend as the affable, generous guru of basketball and life, he would be disappointed in me if I didn't discuss his flaws along with the accolades. There was the man he wanted to be and the man that he was; sometimes the man that he was disappointed him. Sometimes it disappointed me. It is the burden of being great at something that people expect you to be perfect in everything. But his greatness wasn't in being perfect, it was in admitting to his mistakes—and he made some serious ones during the time I knew him—and learning from them.

For me, how he handled those dark episodes is what impressed me the most about him and taught me how to handle my own frequent missteps. Coach had a temper. And he could be stubborn. But how I reacted to him depended upon what stage we were in our relationship.

Our friendship evolved through three distinct stages. Stage I: While I was at UCLA it was a more formal coach–player relationship. We had moments of emotional closeness, but they were fleeting. In part, this was because both of us were reserved, but it was also because I wasn't looking for more. I had just left the home of an overbearing mother and a distant, strict father. I didn't want another judgmental parent. Besides, I was pursuing the wisdom and example of accomplished black men as spiritual guides—like Malcolm X, Muhammad Ali, Martin Luther King, Jr.— not a middle-aged white man with a Midwestern twang who wore white socks with black shoes. What I didn't understand was that during this time Coach was laying the foundation for lifelong lessons that I interpreted as merely practical information on how to become a better basketball player. I recognized that he also cared deeply about me and his other players as more than just transients passing through. He wanted us to leave his charge as mature and capable men with a strong work ethic and stronger moral conscience. Anything less he would have considered a failure on his part. While I appreciated that, I saw myself as a lone wolf on my own adventure.

Stage II includes the years I was playing in the NBA for Milwaukee. I kept in touch with Coach, but I didn't have a tight friendship with him. We occasionally talked on the phone or visited when I was in town. Mostly, he was in my head, an echoing voice that I would hear during practice and in games. But that voice still spoke mostly about basketball. He was my former teacher and I was his ex-student trying to make him proud, while also proving I could make it on my own.

Stage III was our most intimate and rewarding. When I returned to Los Angles to play for the Lakers, we were able to see each other more often, and I got to know him on a much more personal level. By now I was more mature, more confident in who I was as a man and as a player. I could look back on my experiences with Coach and see them the way he looked down on our practices from the top of the Pauley Pavilion. I could now see the bigger picture. I could connect the dots and realize how everything I had learned had affected my actions and choices beyond basketball. Because of that, I was able to show my gratitude to Coach Wooden, and to open myself up to keep learning from him. More, I could repay his influence by being there for him in his times of need, as he was for me. I no longer wanted to impress him, I wanted to support him.

During this latter stage of our friendship, I came to understand, through our candid conversations, just how much pressure I had put on Coach by choosing to attend UCLA. I found out how much one afternoon in his den. We'd been watching the Dodgers putting a big hurt on the Padres. The game was such a blowout that we'd started joking about how the Padres coach was probably in the dugout leafing through retirement brochures for Costa Rica.

"I nearly retired after you left, Kareem," he suddenly told me.

"What?" I said, shocked. "You were at the height of your career. We had put a serious whooping on the world of college basketball."

He nodded and said nothing while watching Dodger Jeff Kent hit a ground ball double. I knew better than to rush Coach. Words were important to him, and he took his time finding the right ones. He often quoted Mark Twain's observation, "The difference between the almost right word and the right word is really a large matter. 'Tis the difference between the lightning bug and the lightning." When Coach spoke, he preferred lightning.

"Before you showed up, we had back-to-back national championships. We had Gail Goodrich, Kenny Washington, and Doug McIntosh—all great players.

Winning both nationals was exciting for the fans because it was not a foregone conclusion. But when you showed up, the popular expectation was that we couldn't lose if we had you. Now winning wasn't just about coaching, it was about getting the big guy the ball. Suddenly we weren't playing to win, we were playing not to lose. I hated that."

Now it was my turn to grope for lightning. I came up with lightning bugs. "I, uh, didn't know."

He shrugged and complained to the TV, "Goodness gracious, son, swing at a pitch already." César Izturis had let two pitches go by, both strikes.

"Thing is, Coach, we never played with the idea of just giving me the ball. Remember when you told me that it would be easy for you to devise an offense that would ensure that I'd be the all-time leading scorer in college history."

"Of course I remember." He grinned. "I was trying to manipulate you into being a team player. Teams with superstar scorers rarely win championships." He turned and looked at me with a smile. "Turns out I didn't have to try very hard. You were already a team player. Remember what you said to me?"

"Was it, 'Quit trying to manipulate me, you old codger'?"

He laughed. "No. I told you we could make you the all-time leading scorer but we wouldn't win championships, and you said, 'Coach, you know I wouldn't want that.'"

He sat back, still smiling at the memory.

"Man, I was awesome," I said.

He laughed again. "You could be. On occasion." He shifted in his chair while we watched a mattress commercial on the TV. His face went serious again. "When you're on top, people expect you to win. They're not satisfied with anything less. And they aren't shy about letting me know. I don't care how good a coach is, he can't stay number one forever."

I just listened. Some days that was the best thing I could do to demonstrate my friendship.

He continued, "You know what I always say, 'I wish all my really good friends in coaching would win one national championship. And those I don't think highly of, I wish they would win several.'"

I realized then that not only was I the source of his greatest triumphs, I was the cause of his greatest anxiety. I felt ashamed that for the four years I played for him, I'd never once given a single thought to the kind of pressure he must have faced. And I looked at him with awe that he'd never once said a single word—lightning or lightning bug—about what he was going through to me or anyone else on the team. The Hemingway line, "Courage is grace under pressure," popped into my head, and I almost said it aloud, because Coach would have been delighted to have me throw a pithy quote at him for a change. But I didn't, because he would have been embarrassed at the compliment.

Instead, I said, "You gonna hog all the peanuts, Coach?"

* * *

Sometimes before practice, Coach would go into the empty gym with team manager Bob Marcucci and just shoot underhand free throws while Bob shagged. At the time, I figured he was just keeping his skills sharp. After all, we all knew about his record of 134 consecutive free throws over 46 games in a row. Looking back, I can see that this routine was probably an attempt to relieve some of the pressure he was under.

That pressure caused some cracks in Coach's relationship with the players and staff. During a trip to Chicago, Bill Sweek played a trick on some teammates with the old bucket-of-water-on-the-door prank. This led to a full-scale water fight that resulted in the hotel manager writing a letter of complaint to the school. Despite the fact that Sidney Wicks and Lynn Shackelford were the instigators, three of the reserve players received the main punishment of being benched for four games. The team couldn't help but notice the unfairness of this from a man who had once said he looked at basketball as a way to teach ethics.

The team also thought Coach was playing favorites with some of his starters, especially me. Other players had to share hotel rooms, but I had my own. While I could see how that might seem like special treatment, it was just a practical solution to the fact that I needed a king-size bed due to my size, and it was rare to find two king-size beds in one hotel room. I always got two glasses of orange juice at breakfast while the others got one, but that too was a concession to my size, not my status. There were other grumblings, sometimes to reporters, about laxness in rules regarding dress, meal attendance, and length of hair. Some of their complaints were justified; Coach had relaxed his rules since I'd arrived. I couldn't feel bad about that. What teenage kid complains when rules are bent for him? But Coach didn't help team unity by telling a player that he was lucky I was on the team because he wouldn't be if I wasn't. "If we have only a few good shoes," he admitted to a reporter, "I guarantee you Lew's going to have good shoes." Coach's justification rang hollow for a man famous for his principles: "I realize I'm not as strict as I used to be, but society isn't as strict, either."

I wasn't even aware of some of the complaints until many years later when I was at a team reunion at Andy Hill's house. Someone was at the bar holding a bottle of vodka, trying to make a screwdriver. "Where's the orange juice?" he asked. "Kareem drank it all," someone answered, and they all laughed. I had no idea why that was funny until Bob Marcucci explained it to me.

Another crack in team unity came in 1968 when Assistant Coach Jerry Norman left UCLA. His public reason was that he needed to earn more money. He was only making $14,000 a year, while Coach Wooden was barely better off with $17,000. By comparison, Dean Smith at the University of North Carolina at Chapel Hill was earning $85,000. But Norman had also made it known that he was frustrated with Coach after comments he'd made after our defeat of Houston. Coach Wooden had told the press that Norman had suggested a box-and-one strategy to contain Houston's powerhouse Elvin Hayes, but that Wooden had changed it to what proved to be the highly successful diamond-and-one. Norman insisted that the strategy had been his idea, and there was a rift that even extended to Norman's wife, June. "She never thought that Jerry got enough credit," Wooden said. "Maybe he didn't, I don't know. It's hard to say. I know I tried personally to always give credit to assistants." Norman left basketball to become a stockbroker, earning $60,000 his first year and eventually becoming a multimillionaire. Coach did publicly give credit to Norman, but the damage was done.

Once during a team photo, Coach went ballistic when a few of the players showed up wearing Adidas shoes rather than the team's Converse-sponsored shoes. He ranted about responsibility and maturity and so on. Everyone knew Coach was good friends with Chuck Taylor, the boss of Converse. However, we also knew that Converse had been such a dominant force in the basketball shoe market that they saw no need to change their designs. Even Coach admitted there was a problem: "Even though my players wore them, I had to use a razor blade myself on every new pair to cut the seam that would be right over the little toe. If I didn't do that, the players would all have blisters." Clearly, Coach struggled with his loyalty to his friend and his loyalty to his players. To us, of course, there should have been no conflict. Finally, Coach came to the same conclusion in 1970 and replaced Converse with Adidas as the team shoe. As soon as I left UCLA to play pro ball with Milwaukee, I became the first person to wear Adidas three-stripe leather shoes.

* * *

Some of the clashes between Coach and the players were much more personal.

Coach's benching of Edgar Lacey after only eleven minutes of our "Game of the Century" with Houston led to Edgar quitting the team, and we lost a key player. My roommate, Lucius Allen, was then suspended for his senior year after his second arrest for marijuana possession. Having lost two valuable members of the team, and having the dunk outlawed, I was starting to feel even more pressure to maintain our winning streak. Before a home game against Washington State,

I was hit with a migraine so severe that the doctor prohibited me from warming up until fifteen minutes before the game started. I was worried that I might miss the game altogether, or that this might become a pattern. The pressure just kept mounting.

Edgar Lacey and Lucius Allen had been close friends. Losing Lucius and Edgar had at first left me a little stressed and depressed. I'd lost two friends, and the team took a broadside. I didn't blame Coach for Edgar's bitter departure—he was the boss and we were there to play how he wanted us to. Now with them gone, the only other black players were Sidney Wicks and Curtis Rowe, both a couple years younger than me, and a lot rowdier and more outgoing. In college, age can be a wider and more treacherous gap than race. So I started to reconnect with other teammates, like Bill Sweek and Mike Lynn, as well as team manager Bob Marcucci. Bob and I bonded over a love of martial arts movies (I had just started training with Bruce Lee) and jazz. "It was very satisfying to reconnect with Kareem," Marcucci later said. "We spent time going to movies and jazz clubs. It was cool." These friendships lifted my spirits to a degree that even the press noticed. "The nonchalance he displays on the court is not new, but his amiable, easygoing manner in public certainly is," Jeff Prugh wrote in the *Los Angeles Times*. "The face lights up in a ready smile. The demeanor is cool, but cordial. The feelings surface more quickly and are expressed sometimes good-humoredly."

That's why it pained me when Bob and Coach finally butted heads. During one of our trips to Washington, Sidney Wicks and a few other players sneaked out of the hotel to attend a party. Since sneaking out had been so easy, they decided to sneak a few girls back in with them. When Coach found out, he gave the culprits a serious dressing-down. Afterward, he scolded Bob for not holding himself to a higher moral standard as part of the coaching staff. Bob argued back, "You have all these double standards!" He proceeded to list them and a few more grievances that had been building up. He expected Coach would kick him off the team right then and there. But he didn't. He just nodded and said, "Okay, Bob, go to practice."

I was as surprised as Bob when he told me. Yet, at the same time, I wasn't. Coach could get as heated as the next person, but in the end, he was ruled by decency, fairness, and rationality. Even Bob later said, "One of the most amazing things about Coach was that he did listen to people, even in the heat of battle."

The most shocking incident I ever witnessed with Coach Wooden was at the national semifinals in Louisville. We'd been winning all our games, but Coach had noticed a certain lack of energy lately from the team, which he feared was complacency. It showed that night as we struggled to maintain a slim lead over the feisty Bulldogs. Coach's mood was tense, so when Bill Sweek made a defensive error in the first half, Coach yanked him from the game. Sweek sat on the bench fuming. He was a senior and had played eighty-nine games as a Bruin. Pulling him seemed like an overly harsh move to Sweek. When John Vallely fouled out with only four minutes left, Coach gestured for Sweek to go in. Sweek decided to demonstrate his displeasure with Coach by slowly swaggering to the table. Coach responded with a brusque "Sit down!" and sent in Terry Schofield instead. Sweek was so incensed that he marched straight out of the gym and to the locker room.

I was on the court at the time, not noticing any of this drama. We pulled off the win by only three points, sending us to the national finals. The team hurried into the locker room relieved with the win. Once there, I started undressing to shower. That's when I heard the shouting.

"Goodness gracious, what were you thinking, Bill?" Coach barked.

"That you shouldn't have pulled me from the game!"

"You don't know what you're talking about. You have no idea what I do."

"Just because I don't have 'Coach' in front of my name doesn't mean I don't know basketball!"

Wearing only my shorts, I padded barefoot around

the locker to see Coach Wooden being held by both arms by assistant coaches Gary Cunningham and Denny Crum. Sweek was still in the shower room, a towel around his waist, his chin jutting at Coach in defiance. Coach looked like he was going to launch at him with both fists.

"You wanna fight me, old man? You've been messing with my mind for five years!" Sweek hollered.

Some of the guys laughed, but the rest of us just stared with mouths open. We had never seen Coach this angry before.

"In fact, you're always right," Sweek continued. "Edgar Lacey quit, but you were right, and he was wrong. Don Saffer quit, but you were right, and he was wrong. All these problems, and you're just never wrong. Did you ever think the problem was you?"

Coach seemed to calm down at that. He turned and walked out, making sure that reporters were kept out so no one could leak what had just happened.

Sweek rode the team bus back to the hotel, convinced that not only was he off the team, but he might be out of UCLA.

I sided with Coach on this dispute. Sweek was always trying to push the boundaries that Coach set. I didn't mind players letting Coach know when they disagreed with him. That was reasonable and even beneficial for team morale. But Sweek seemed to delight in pushing buttons until Coach's face tightened into that gray mask that warned he'd reached his limit, not one step further.

Friday morning we all went to breakfast. I'm guessing I had two orange juices while everyone else had one. Sweek figured he'd squeeze one more breakfast out of the campus budget before being sent packing. Toward the end of the meal, Coach came in and told us he wanted to have a word with us. We gritted our teeth, expecting Coach's terrible swift sword would fall on Sweek's head.

"I've given a lot of hard thought to what Bill said last night," Coach said. His voice was quiet but firm. Resolute. "I can see that what Bill said was not altogether without merit."

Sweek nearly did a spit-take of his water. He looked at Coach cautiously, as if he was expecting security to rush in and drag him out of the room.

"Now, I certainly don't agree with the way he delivered his opinions, or his behavior on the court, any more than I condone the way I reacted. But I'm glad we got it all out in the open."

We stared quietly. Not a fork or knife touched a plate.

"Anyway," Coach said, "I just want you to know how proud I am of all of you..." When he said "all," he looked straight at Sweek. "And how happy I am to have the privilege of coaching you." He nodded at Sweek. "Come here, Bill."

Sweek got up and walked tentatively to Coach. Coach stuck out his hand, and Sweek flinched, just a little. Then he smiled and they shook hands, and the rest of us let out a deep internal sigh of relief.

I was not surprised by the outcome of their spat. Based on everything I knew about his personality and his character, it was mathematically inevitable that Coach would take to heart what one of his players said, feel compelled to patch things up, and teach us all a lesson in humility at the same time. Other coaches would have felt the need to stand up to Sweek to prove to everyone who was in charge. But we already knew who was in charge, and it was moments like this that made us glad it was Coach.

That day left a lasting impression on us. Bob Marcucci later remarked how he was "just stunned that Wooden would be so honest about how he cared for the team. Other than his wife and kids, he was not open to talking about his feelings that way. He didn't want to burden other people. It made a real impression on everybody." Sweek was particularly impressed: "I think most coaches would have thrown me off the team. We were under all this pressure—I know he felt the pressure—but despite all that, and despite what I had done, the fact that he would try to bring us together and mend this thing and forgive me I thought was impressive. He forgave me and wanted me to be there and play in the final game."

I'm sure the public would have liked to imagine us all as one big, happy family. Well, in most ways we were. We couldn't have been that successful that long without sharing mutual respect and affection. But like any family that spends every day together under intense pressure and public scrutiny, there were disagreements. To expect the coach to have to wrangle a bunch of turbo-charged, highly competitive athletes riding the ego high of being the best team in the country without getting occasionally irked is expecting him to have supernatural powers. I preferred the humble man of principle who struggled to do the right thing despite enormous soul-crushing pressure, despite self-doubt, despite stumbling when trying to live up to his own high standards. I preferred his grace under pressure.

*　*　*

After graduating, I moved to Milwaukee to play for the Bucks and finally live my life as an adult. Because of Coach Wooden, I left UCLA a basketball player able to play on a professional level. At the time, I thought that basketball was the most important thing he had taught me. Like most kids leaving the cocoon of college, I had no idea what I'd actually learned. That would come with time. During my six years in Milwaukee, I had plenty of opportunity to look back on my years with Coach Wooden and have numerous aha moments when

I would stop and think, "Oh, so that's what he meant." It reminded me of the old saying that Coach quoted when he thought we weren't listening to him: "When I was a boy of fourteen, my father was so ignorant I could hardly stand to have the old man around. But when I got to be twenty-one, I was astonished at how much the old man had learned in seven years."

During this time I called Coach every so often, just to keep in touch. When I played in Los Angeles, I visited him. We were friendly, but not yet close friends. He was still my old teacher, and I was the young basketball star eager to prove how much I'd grown on my own. Our conversations were mostly about basketball, a mixture of me telling him about my experiences in the pros and us reminiscing about our time playing together.

"You know, Kareem," he said during one of my visits, "I've always wondered something about that last game at Pauley with USC."

"Last regular-season game," I reminded him.

"It was only your second loss with me."

"Believe me, I remember." That loss ended a fifty-one-game streak at Pauley Pavilion and a seventeen-game streak over USC.

"I felt bad because your dad was there. Didn't he play trombone with the UCLA band that day?"

"*First* trombone, as he reminded me."

"Right. First trombone." He tore open a packet of crackers that came with his tomato soup. He carefully removed them from the wrapper as if they were radioactive. "I've always felt bad about that loss."

"Only our second loss out of ninety games, Coach," I reminded him. I was trying to sound upbeat about it, but the truth was it bothered me, too. The fact that it bothered me also bothered me. I was in the pros now, with more important things to think about than one stupid college game. I had become the first player to be named the NCAA tournament's Most Outstanding Player three times. We had earned three NCAA titles together in a row. That one game didn't matter. Why was he bringing it up over grilled cheese sandwiches and tomato soup?

"What did you wonder?" I asked him. "You said you always wondered something about that game."

"Well, I always wondered if you were planning to dunk that game. I heard a rumor that you were planning to throw one down just to defy the rules committee that banned it. Is that true?"

"Is that why you pulled me out of the game with only two minutes left?"

He didn't answer. "Were you?"

I shook my head. "I'd thought about it. It would have been sweet to jam one. Kind of a *Shaft* moment."

"A what?"

I smiled. "An in-your-face moment. But I decided not to. I made thirty-seven points that game and twenty rebounds. I think that made my point." I didn't tell him that I also didn't want to embarrass him.

He nodded. "I pulled you so you wouldn't get injured before the playoffs. That would be your legacy."

"Our legacy," I corrected.

He shrugged. "Legacy," he said, as if he'd never spoken the word before. "Not the reason we play, though, is it?"

I didn't say anything. I didn't want to be rude by disagreeing. But, yeah, legacy was part of the reason I played. I liked the idea of breaking records, surpassing other players, having my name in record books. It was not the main reason I played, but the thought of it was definitely at the back of my mind; it's at the back of every young player's mind.

"I'm glad you didn't dunk that day," Coach said, pointing a cracker at me. "But if you had, that would have been something to remember." He grinned mischievously, like a kid who'd just toilet-papered the principal's house.

That surprised me. "You would have been livid."

"Absolutely. But that would have been my story, not yours. My legacy, not yours."

We changed subjects, but I kept thinking about what he had said. I was still a young player in the pros. I was confident in my playing ability, but I was still figuring out everything else: my future, my family, my religion, my politics, and how to balance it all. I had recently changed my name and was enduring the nasty backlash. Coach knew all that from our conversations and the news reports. Now he was reminding me to choose the path that best suited me. Not him, not the public, not my parents, not anyone else. That would be my legacy.

I left the restaurant that day with two things: a tomato soup stain on my shirt, and the realization that the legacy I had with Coach wasn't over, it was just starting. It was not a legacy that would appear in any record books. Sports analysts would never refer to it on TV shows. My obituary would not mention it. But our legacy as friends would be one of the most important and rewarding accomplishments of my life.

* * *

I returned to Los Angeles in 1975 to play with the Lakers, just in time for Coach Wooden's retirement. It's just possible that I took his retirement harder than he did. To me, it was like having your parents sell your childhood home. Yes, UCLA would still be there, but the campus wasn't my home, Coach was. His love had been unconditional, his support unending.

"Coach, are you sure about this?"

"It's time, Lewis." He usually called me Kareem. This seemed like a nostalgic slip.

I was torn between congratulating him and trying to talk him out of it. Of course, I realized I wanted him to stay for selfish reasons, so I could step back into my past at any time and everything would still be as it was. I wanted to revisit my childhood home and find my room just as I left it.

"Congratulations, Coach. Well deserved."

"I'm not dying, for goodness sake. I'm only sixty-four. I've got my summer camps, books, speaking engagements. My daily five-mile walks. Nell and I are going on a Caribbean cruise."

"You're busier than I am," I said, forcing myself to sound upbeat. "Plus, you just won your tenth NCAA championship. I guess I'll have to stop taking credit for your success."

He laughed. "Oh, Kareem."

I don't know why those two words touched me so much at that moment. I liked to make him laugh. It's how I told him I cared about him, that he mattered to me.

"I did my best," Coach said. "Any time you can walk away saying you did your best, you've won."

"Sure, of course." Words were coming out of my mouth, but I wasn't saying them. I wanted to say positive things.

"Don't worry, I'll be fine. Everything is just as I want it."

I called to congratulate him and he ended up comforting me. Classic Coach Wooden.

I sighed. "I could use a good quote right about now, Coach. A poem, a book, a fortune cookie?"

He thought for a moment, undoubtedly riffling through the collection in his mind, undoubtedly filed according to theme. Finally, he said, "Th-Th-that's all, folks."

I laughed.

* * *

I found my own appropriate quote shortly after that phone call. From Papa Hemingway himself: "As you get older, it's more difficult to have heroes, but it's just as necessary." It was with that in mind that I attended Coach's sixty-fifth birthday extravaganza at Pauley Pavilion. With all the celebrities there you would have thought it was the Oscars. Bob Hope, the emcee of many Oscar shows, was the emcee here as well. Frank Sinatra was crooning some of his most popular songs. Many of Coach's former players were there, including Gail Goodrich and my old roommate, Lucius Allen.

Los Angeles mayor Tom Bradley was at the party, declaring the day "John Wooden Day." UCLA presented Coach with a blue Mercedes-Benz, a gold watch studded with ten diamonds to represent his ten NCAA titles, and four lifetime tickets to UCLA home games. It was easy to know which gift held the most value to Coach. He would soon trade in the Mercedes for a much more modest sedan. I rarely saw the watch. But he would attend many UCLA games; some of them we attended together.

Coach finally took to the podium to thank everyone. "This is the most memorable evening of my athletic career," he said. "The two great loves of my life are my family and UCLA." He spoke about his life at UCLA, the teams he'd coached, the boys who had turned into such decent and accomplished men. Then he waved for Nell to come up. "You have always been with me since I would see you up there in the high school band holding a trumpet." Then, looking out at his players gathered to honor him, a slight catch in his throat, he continued, "Next to my family, I feel closest to my players. I am sorry if I ever hurt any of them. I never meant to. There is no player I haven't loved."

"Jesus," I heard one of his players mutter behind me, choking up.

"Yeah," another whispered, struggling not to do the same.

And that was it. The end of an era. Of a legacy. Of a time when the best freshman basketball players in the country were taught how to put on their shoes and socks. When academics was more important than scoring. When moral character was taught along with lay-up and passing drills.

I have walked the UCLA campus many times since that day, including just a week before this writing. And every time, I half expect to see Coach hurrying along the sidewalk, a whistle around his neck, his perfectly coiffed hair reflecting a perfect sun.

* * *

After a couple years of me living in Los Angeles, Coach and I fell into a routine of phone calls, meals, and den-sitting. Eating at restaurants was tricky because people would spot my head poking up toward the lighting fixture, then they'd see Coach's gray hair, combed into a perfect representation of a freshly plowed field. Over they'd come to ask for an autograph, photo, or just to say thanks for all the pleasure we'd given them over the years.

I admit that I was quicker to annoyance than Coach. Try finishing a patty melt when someone interrupts every bite. The trick is to order cold sandwiches because the hot ones are never hot by the time you get to them. However, Coach was always gracious and friendly, making each person feel like a welcomed interruption of his otherwise bland day. Seeing the joyful look on fans' faces when they walked away made me copy his behavior. But for me it was like trying to learn a complicated dance step by watching a Fred Astaire movie. Looks easy, but ain't. I knew part of the reason was racial. He never had to worry about some racist coming up to call him a name or do him bodily harm. He could afford to see the good in everybody. I couldn't. But he made me try.

One afternoon we were sitting in a restaurant discussing why my baseball picks were clearly far superior to his. He stubbornly disagreed, trying to sway me with facts and statistics. I was enjoying refusing to acknowledge his points. In the middle of our discussion, and three signed autographs into lunch, a thin man with a thinner mustache approached the table. He was smiling, so Coach and I smiled back.

"Hi, Coach," the man said. He nodded at me. "Kareem."

"Good afternoon," Coach said.

"I was just wondering..." the thin man began.

Coach and I both stiffened in our seats. Fans who started with "I was wondering" always ended that sentence with criticism. The thin man held true to form.

"...why it took you so long to win your first national championship?"

Coach had been a coach at Indiana State from 1946 to 1948 before starting at UCLA in 1948. He won his first NCAA Division I Tournament title in

Coach proudly displays his Pyramid of Success in 1964. When it came to basketball—and life—no one knew more about success. (UCLA Photography, a division of Associated Students UCLA)

UCLA, in 1965, shows their appreciation for Coach's second consecutive national championship. (UCLA Photography, a division of Associated Students UCLA)

Coach gives me a rare break from the action. He's sitting straight, focused but relaxed. I'm leaning forward, anxious to get back in. That was our basic posture for all our games together. (Bill Ray/GETTY)

Coach shows off his ball-handling skills while at Purdue University, c. 1929.

UCLA vs. Notre Dame in my sophomore year in 1966. We look like we're re-enacting the Jets walk in *West Side Story*. "When you're a Bruin, you're a Bruin all the way..." (Bill Ray/GETTY)

1966-67 Season Team Photo. I definitely look happiest, maybe because I know we're going to end the season 30-0 and win a third consecutive national championship. (UCLA Photography, a division of Associated Students UCLA)

UCLA vs. USC during the 1966-67 season. We beat them every game for the four years I was at UCLA—except my very last game in my senior year. A pity loss? (UCLA Photography, a division of Associated Students UCLA)

Coach gives us advice, which you can bet we followed. (UCLA Photography, a division of Associated Students UCLA)

Although this looks like one of our opponents tried to burn this 1967 photo out of frustration, it actually was singed when my Bel Air home burned to the ground in 1983. (UCLA Photography, a division of Associated Students UCLA)

Teammate Mike Warren, me, and Coach at the end of the 1967 season awards banquet. For some reason, Coach's award is smaller than ours. (UCLA Photography, a division of Associated Students UCLA)

Blocking a Minnesota shot in my sophomore year. Might be part of the reason we won 95-55. (Norm Levin, Natural Portraits & Events)

Coach leads us to another NCAA championship in 1968. (UCLA Photography, a division of Associated Students UCLA)

Coach and I celebrate my Most Valuable Player award after defeating St. John's University in 1968. (Bettmann/GETTY)

1969 cover photo for *Sports Illustrated*. While I was thrilled by the honor, I was just as pleased that it honored all the Coach Wooden had taught me. (Rick Clarkson/GETTY)

Coach hands me a couple trophies at the 1969 UCLA Basketball Awards Ceremony at the school's Pauley Pavilion. The sunglasses and goatee were part of my jazzman look. (Bettman/GETTY)

Bill Walton, Coach, and me at my 50th birthday party in 1997. (Deborah Morales)

President George W. Bush presents Coach with the Presidential Medal of Freedom Award in 2003. (Alex Wong/GETTY)

Thirteen years after Coach received his, I receive the Presidential Medal of Freedom. Coach forged the path that so many of his players followed. I followed his path to the White House. (Bettmann/GETTY)

Coach and I in Chicago in 2005 where I interviewed him on camera for my documentary about the Harlem Renaissance, *On the Shoulders of Giants*. He considered the Harlem Rens the best basketball team he'd ever played against. (Deborah Morales)

In 1998, former UCLA player Keith Erickson and I were on hand when Coach became the first basketball figure inducted into the Los Angeles Memorial Coliseum's Court of Honor which "commemorates outstanding persons or events, athletic or otherwise, that have had a definite impact upon the history, glory and growth of the Los Angeles Memorial Coliseum." (Deborah Morales)

Coach in his den in 2008. From this angle you can only see a small portion of the mementoes that decorated the most famous den in Los Angeles. (Sporting News Archive/GETTY)

Coach's favorite booth at VIP's where we spent many a meals pondering the mysteries of the universe. (Paul Ma)

Coach and I at his Encino home in 2009. He's trying to find out how it feels to be taller than me. (Deborah Morales)

The UCLA Anderson School of Management offers a John Wooden Global Leadership Award in 2010 "for exemplary leadership and service to the community." Here Coach and I are on a panel discussing the role of leadership in society. (from l-r: Deborah Roberts of ABC News, Coach Wooden, Kareem Abdul-Jabbar, Keith Erickson and Jamaal Wilkes). (Deborah Morales)

Coach in his classic courtside expression of strategizing the next move. (From the lens of George Kalinsky)

The greatest coach in basketball history. (UCLA Photography, a division of Associated Students UCLA)

Coach and I have a contest to see who looks better with a shirt collar. You decide. (Deborah Morales)

We also compete to see who looks better in a tux. His snazzy vest gives him the edge. (The Private Collection of Nan Wooden)

This is the serious, focused face that we players were used to during a game. (UCLA Photography, a division of Associated Students UCLA)

This photo defines Coach. He's hugging his beloved wife, clutching a stack of books, and wearing an awful gaudy tie. (UCLA Photography, a division of Associated Students UCLA)

Mike Warren, me, and Bill Walton, celebrate Coach's 97th birthday at Andy Hill's house. (Alexandra Berman)

One of the many times we got together to celebrate our 1967 team history together. (UCLA Photography, a division of Associated Students UCLA)

1964, eighteen years after starting his coaching career. The question was meant to show off the thin man's knowledge as well as put Coach on the defensive. It was the kind of fan confrontation that I had parodied in the movie *Airplane!* when the little boy tells me his dad says I don't work hard enough on defense.

Coach looked up at the thin man and smiled even wider. "I admit I am a slow learner. But you notice that when I learn something, I have it down pretty good."

The thin man's thin smile faded, and he walked away.

Coach returned to his sandwich as if nothing had happened.

"How long you been holding on to that comeback, Coach?" I asked.

"What makes you think this is the first time I've used it?"

I laughed. I should have known it wasn't the first time someone had asked him that question. Sometimes I imagined him sitting in his den, writing down one-liners for later use. I'd heard what he'd said to Marques Johnson when they were discussing the 1975 NCAA final. Coach told him that he'd played twenty-seven minutes that game. Marques thought it was a lot less. To which Coach replied, "The way you played, you weren't the only one who didn't realize you were out there."

Marques and everyone around them had laughed.

"Maybe you should switch from writing about your Pyramid of Success to an Octagon of Snappy Retorts," I suggested.

"Maybe you should pick up the check today."

"See, that's exactly what I mean."

He gave me a look. I picked up the check.

* * *

My friendship with Coach changed dramatically when I began coaching in 1998. Until then, we'd spend time watching baseball games or basketball games on TV, or having meals at restaurants near his home, or we'd talk on the phone about movies or TV shows. It was all very casual conversation but spiced with affection. Much of what I learned from Coach during these years was through things he told me directly, the examples he set, or just osmosis.

Coach was filled with quotes from poems and famous successful people about the qualities necessary for a fulfilling life. Eventually, he distilled all of his teachings into a handy Pyramid of Success. There are too many elements to that pyramid to do it justice here, but suffice it to say that I was very aware of adapting them to my own life. The two ascending sides of the pyramid emphasized faith and patience. Regarding faith, my adherence to Islam had not diminished over the years since my conversion, but I had modified it from the intense orthodoxy I had followed at first to a more streamlined version that I felt was more progressive and inclusive. I practiced quietly on my own without the need to proselytize. I had been able to separate my faith in the theology from using it to make a cultural statement about black Americans. My only interest in Islam was spiritual and ethical guidance, not politics.

In part, I credited my relaxed attitude toward my religion to observing Coach's attitude toward Christianity. He was devout, reading the Bible daily, and regularly attending the First Christian Church. But he also followed his own pyramid teaching of adaptability. He focused on the qualities of the kind of man he wanted to be, which included reliability, integrity, honesty, and sincerity—then he adapted his behavior to achieve those goals rather than worrying about every line in the Bible. It was a lot like the way he coached basketball: Don't worry about set plays; instead, have the fundamentals down, and you can adapt to each circumstance to achieve the desired outcome—doing good. That made a lot of sense to me, and I soon did the same thing: focused less on following the words and more on being the words. Don't follow the teaching on being compassionate, practice compassion until you can't help but be that way when it's called for. It was jazz as religion: everyone playing the same song, but adapting, improvising, harmonizing until we produced beautiful music together.

The other edge of the pyramid featured patience, which Coach demonstrated in abundance. When players insisted on trying some new move or shot that he didn't approve of, he made his case against it. If the player still wasn't convinced, he let them do it their way. The end result almost always proved Coach to be right. But patience taught the lesson without any animosity or resentment. During my time in the pros, I found it easy to be patient. I had the confidence (another of Coach's pyramid building blocks) that came with practicing skills and continually winning to be certain I would get what I want. Patience was easy because I hadn't had a lot of experience with disappointment. However, in the five years leading up to 1998, my patience was seriously challenged.

After retiring from playing professional basketball in 1989, I'd taken a few years off from the sport. A cleansing of the palate. But after my mother's death in 1997, I was antsy to get back on the court, not as a player but as a coach. Her death had left me feeling unmoored, and I needed to do something I was good at. I needed a purpose.

It was Coach Wooden who first suggested coaching to me. "I think you'd make a fine coach. You've always been a leader."

I was confident that I would quickly be snatched up. I had retired as the all-time leader in points scored (38,387), games played (1,560), minutes played

(57,446), field goal attempts (28,307), blocked shots (3,189), and defensive rebounds (9,394) and a whole lot of career awards for best this and all-star that. I knew all the fundamentals of basketball, and I knew how to win. *Line up, boys,* I thought, *who wants first crack at Coach Kareem.*

Teams were very polite, but the end result was always the same: nothing but *nyet.*

Coach had reached out to Chancellor Charles Young at UCLA about hiring me. Chancellor Young was very agreeable to the suggestion, but before anything could be formalized, he retired, and the new chancellor was not as enthusiastic.

"Coach, I can't find a single team who wants me," I complained during a desperate phone call.

"What reason are they giving you?" Coach asked.

"Lack of coaching experience. As if thirty years of playing at the highest level isn't experience enough."

"Playing's not the same as coaching," he said. "You know that."

"I know. But given my experience, I can learn pretty—" I was about to spit out an expletive, but caught myself just in time. "—pretty darn quickly."

"Magic Johnson and Bill Russell didn't do too well when they coached. I'm sure that's in the back of their heads."

"I'd like to put something in the back of their heads," I groused. I was taking self-pity up to the next level.

Coach would not indulge self-pity. "Your arrests didn't help, I'm sure."

"One arrest. And one fine." I had been arrested for accosting a motorist who'd blocked traffic and flipped me off while I was on the way to visit my terminally ill mother to authorize ending her life support. Granted, I hadn't been in the right mood to handle confrontation at the time and I'd acted like a jerk. I was sentenced to anger management classes. The fine was for carrying a small amount of marijuana, which I used to lessen the debilitating migraine headaches that had plagued me since childhood. I paid a five-hundred-dollar fine. I didn't say all that because Coach didn't like excuses, even good ones.

"Look, they say you don't have experience," Coach said. "Then get some."

"I think that's the point of this conversation, Coach. I can't get a coaching job because I don't have experience and I can't get experience because I can't get a coaching job. Catch-twenty-two."

"I didn't say it would be easy." There was no sympathy in his voice, and I wasn't in the mood for tough love.

"Where's that on your Pyramid?" I tried not to sound obnoxious; I failed.

He didn't miss a beat. "Initiative. Second row up."

Sometimes our conversations didn't end with unicorns and puppies, but with fingernails dragged across half a mile of chalkboard.

* * *

But Coach was right. I needed to take initiative and get some coaching experience. Any kind, anywhere. I was mulling over some places to try when I received a call from John Clark, the superintendent of Whiteriver Unified School District Number 20 on the Fort Apache reservation in the White Mountains of Arizona. "You wouldn't help coach our basketball team, would you?" Clark asked.

I resisted shouting, "Hell, yeah!" and instead said somberly, "Yes, I would."

The call was not totally out of the blue. I had visited the area four years earlier when I had been doing research for a book I wanted to write about the Buffalo Soldiers, the black cavalry members who served in the West after the Civil War and were stationed only five miles south of Whiteriver. I had been studying Western history for years and was an avid collector of Western artifacts, from weapons to clothing to rugs. I felt an affinity with Native Americans because they shared some of the same indignities that had been forced on African-Americans. During that trip, I'd made friends with Edgar Perry, cultural adviser to the tribe. I even accepted Edgar's invitation to dance at the puberty ceremony for a young girl in his family. Knowing I felt a special bond with his people, and that I was looking to coach, he suggested they ask me about coaching at Alchesay High School.

It wasn't long before I was on the phone with Coach Wooden.

"I thought you knew what to do. I seem to recall something about 'thirty years of playing at the highest level is experience enough.'"

He wasn't going to make this easy. "Just need a little review. Refresh my memory sort of thing. The ball goes through the hoop, right?"

He laughed heartily. "Oh, Kareem, you know I'd be happy to help you."

And help me he did. He discussed everything from his drills to skills to coaching philosophy to player personalities. "Don't forget the socks," he added. "No blisters."

My calls to Coach continued over the next seven years as I went on to be head coach for the Oklahoma Storm of the United States Basketball League in 2002, winning the league championship, then when I went on to scout for the New York Knicks, then as a special assistant to Lakers head coach Phil Jackson, where I worked with the team's centers, particularly a young, unseasoned rookie, Andrew Bynum.

In 2005, the Lakers drafted seventeen-year-old Andrew Bynum straight out of high school, making him the youngest player to be drafted in NBA history. At seven feet tall, he had the potential to be a dominant player. But his talent was raw, and the transition from playing high schoolers to playing against seasoned pros is profound. Lakers coach Phil Jackson hired me to help Andrew make that transition. I started with Coach Wooden's basic teachings: Learn the fundamentals, be better conditioned than anyone else, focus the mind of achieving peak performance, not on winning the game. Andrew was receptive at first, and his game improved significantly. But eventually he became impatient and wanted to do things his way, as is typical for someone so young and inexperienced. Remembering my own cockiness at that age, I tried even harder to help him develop the basic skills he needed to continue improving. To some degree—certainly not completely— I was successful. In 2012, Andrew was traded.

I especially relied on Coach's advice with respect to the politics of coaching, where I had no experience.

While coaching at Oklahoma, I called Coach late one night after a grueling day. "Sorry, Coach, you awake?"

"One eye is."

I released a flurry of questions and problems I was having, not the least of which was that the team owner wanted me to play his friend's son, who was not a good player.

"The coach is the face of the team. You have to protect them. Does playing this kid protect them?"

"No. But I finally have a head coach job, and I don't want to lose it. I know that's selfish, but it was a steep climb getting here." I had already had one run-in with the owner when I pulled a player he liked. The guy could shoot three-pointers beautifully in practice when no one was guarding him, but in the game with a hand in his face he rarely made one. That argument hadn't gone well.

"I understand, Kareem, I really do. No one would blame you for playing him for a few minutes and taking him out again."

"No one but the rest of the team."

He didn't say anything to that. He didn't have to.

* * *

During my coaching years, Coach Wooden and I advanced from casual buddies to a much richer and deeper friendship. We shared on a completely different level now. He was still helping me—not as a teacher, but as a colleague. Like two soldiers who had been through the same battles together.

I could feel the difference whenever I went to sit with him in his den. Before, it had felt like I was visiting a friend. Now it felt like I was coming home.

Chapter 6

"Time Can Bend Your Knees"

The Hours of Friendship in the Days of Grief

"Friendship is two-sided. It isn't a friend just because someone's doing something nice for you. That's a nice person. There's friendship when you do for each other. It's like marriage—it's two-sided."

—*John Wooden*

Coach Wooden and I shared our lives for more than four decades. During that time, I learned many useful lessons from him that brightened my life. But some experiences are so dark and so personal that they don't easily lend themselves to quotable one-line lessons. In those times, we are less interested in learning than in just surviving. Friendship helps you through those times, not because a friend offers wise words or insights about life, but because a friend is there beside you, providing comfort and strength just by their presence.

Grief is the true challenge of a friendship, and Coach and I faced plenty of those challenges over the years.

The older you get, the larger a role death plays in the story of your life. Friends and loved ones die. Your health begins to deteriorate until your own fragile mortality stares at you every time you look into the mirror. Death is no longer a slow traveler on a distant continent, but an annoying stalker hanging around on the street corner outside your window.

Coach Wooden lived for ninety-nine years, so in his later years, death was no longer content stalking and had become a constant companion. His former players died, his friends died, his colleagues died, his wife, Nell, died. I was thirty-seven years younger than Coach, but over our years together, I had endured death's unwelcome intrusion several times myself: the brutal murders of friends in a house I owned, the untimely death of my old martial arts teacher and close friend Bruce Lee at age thirty-two, the death of my mother, and a few years after that, the death of my father following years of dementia.

"Time can bend your knees / Time can break your heart," Eric Clapton observes in "Tears in Heaven," his song about the death of his young son. Coach and I both had our knees bent and our hearts broken. The worst effect of death is how it isolates the survivors from life. Though our friends and family reach out to comfort us, we tend to retreat into ourselves to wrestle with our dark and heavy grief until we can defeat it. We will forever bear the ugly scars of that struggle, but we can then rejoin our community to begin the healing process.

Coach and I did our best to help each other through these life-altering deaths, to descend into the dark cave of each other's grief, take the other by the hand, and guide him back up to the light. Sure, there were life lessons that we would be able to articulate years later when the pain could be put in perspective. But the only thing that mattered at the time was that we were present in each other's lives. A hand to hold, feet to follow up out of the darkness.

* * *

I was twenty-five in 1973 when a double tragedy struck me with such force that I thought I might never recover. Ironically, the first tragedy was at a house I owned in Washington, D.C., on January 18. I was married with a baby and deep into my studies of Islam. My spiritual teacher, Hamaas Abdul Khaalis, had taught me how to be a Muslim, and I had looked upon him with the same love and respect as I had Coach Wooden. But where Coach had, if not encouraged, at least endured his players speaking their minds, Hamaas was a rigid despot when it came to the teachings of Islam. My curiosity and devotion had led me to explore other teachers and their writings, even taking a summer course in Arabic at Harvard University, and I discovered that many learned clergy disagreed with Hamaas's beliefs. Where Coach had been pleased by exploration of faith, even though it wasn't his, Hamaas became violently angry at my extracurricular studies. "If you don't want to follow the way I teach you," he warned, "you can go and do whatever it is you want to do."

"But—" I protested.

He cut me off with a menacing scowl. "If you don't think we're correct, we're leaving the house."

I agonized for days about what to do. I didn't yet have the confidence to go against my spiritual leader. It would be like a priest telling the pope he didn't know what he was talking about. I chose to hand over the house to Hamaas and his followers.

A few months later, on January 18, 1973, I was back in Milwaukee attending practice with the Bucks. When I got home, I answered a call from the secretary at the Bucks' front office telling me something terrible had happened in D.C., and they were being deluged by press from all over the world. I soon found out that in retaliation for letters Hamaas had written to the Black Muslims' Elijah Muhammad in which he called him a false prophet, a group of eight or nine armed thugs had attacked the house. Hamaas was not home at the time, but they nevertheless proceeded to murder seven people, including Hamaas's three sons, one of whom was ten years old. They also shot his wife and daughter in the head, although both survived. In their final act of barbarism, the killers drowned three infants in the bathtub and sink.

Police arrived at my house the next morning to provide twenty-four-hour protection against any further attacks by the Black Muslims. I was scared for my wife, Habiba, and our baby, and I was grateful for the police presence. I returned to Washington, D.C., to be a pallbearer at the funerals. Hamaas, who had been my main source of comfort and support since leaving UCLA and Coach Wooden, was himself too enraged and grief-stricken to accept my offer of friendship and help. Instead, he barricaded himself inside the house and surrounded it with armed guards.

For months afterward, I traveled with a police escort whenever I was in a city that had a significant population of Black Muslims. Living in constant fear for my family and myself forced me into near paranoia. I cut myself off from everything and everyone that I absolutely didn't have to be exposed to. In some ways, I had become more like Hamaas than I wanted to admit.

Coach Wooden made several attempts to contact me, but I didn't respond. The outside world was a threat to us, and no one out there could understand what we were going through. That included Coach Wooden, an aging white guy whose harshest language was "for goodness sake." I didn't care one bit about his Pyramid of Success, or aphorisms, or literary quotes about life and death and God's plan. I didn't need that, I didn't want that. What I wanted was to hear his voice, to hear the kindness and compassion so I could believe that those things still existed in this screwed-up world where children were drowned over theological differences.

But I just couldn't bring myself to reach out to hear that voice, maybe because I knew that any hope I would get from him would be a lie. Sure, he believed in the goodness of people, just as he had told me on the drive home from the Bat Rack, where the old woman had called me a nigger. If he wanted to go through life in rose-colored glasses, let him. But my glasses were blood-colored. I saw people for what they really were.

In an effort to recover my faith, I decided to leave America to travel through the Middle East to continue my exploration of Islam. I visited Libya, Saudi Arabia, Iran, Afghanistan, Thailand, and Malaysia. I immersed myself in Muslim culture, even speaking my broken Arabic as much as possible. My faith was cautiously returning. I was anxious to return home to share my renewed faith with my family.

On the way home, I decided to stop off in Hong Kong to visit my old martial arts teacher and friend, Bruce Lee. I had met Bruce while still a student at UCLA. His energetic teaching style and astonishing physical prowess pulled me right in. We started as teacher and student, but quickly became friends. He was only seven years older than me, not the thirty-seven years older that Coach Wooden was. Bruce even invited me to be a villain in his movie *Game of Death*. After everything I had been through, I was excited to see my old friend and for us to catch up on each other's lives. When I landed in Singapore on July 20 to catch a connecting flight to Hong Kong, I heard the news. Bruce Lee was dead.

My arrival in the U.S. was not the triumphant return I had hoped for. The tragedies had taken too great a toll on both my wife and me. We became recluses, rarely leaving our home, mostly studying the Qur'an and listening to music. Hamaas had brought us together and, in a way, he was rending us apart. Five months after I returned, we decided to divorce.

I thought about calling Coach, just to tell him what was happening. But part of me was embarrassed. I felt that I had left UCLA for a career in the pros as a towering hero that he could be proud of. And I had adopted Islam and taken political stances for the black community that I could be proud of. Now I felt as if I had failed on some spiritual level. I had fallen from grace.

Another part of me just didn't want another teacher, even a former one. One teacher had nearly been murdered, the other was dead. For his own health and safety, Coach would be better off keeping his distance from me right now.

Looking back, I regret not calling Coach. His calm presence was a spiritual balm. Sitting in a chair in his den, you could sometimes feel your anxiety seeping out of your body into the worn fabric. But I was too young, too proud, too wounded to go to him.

* * *

Our next encounter with death came twelve years later, in 1985. The love story between Coach and his wife, Nell, will be some future generation's *The Notebook*, to be swooned and cried over for lifetimes to come. The up-and-coming actors who play them will be instantly catapulted into stardom, but no matter what roles or awards they win afterward, they will forever be remembered for playing John and Nell Wooden. To everyone who knew them, their love was the stuff dreams are made of.

Nell and Coach met in high school when he was fourteen years old. Nell, in order to watch the handsome basketball star John Wooden, talked her way into the school band by convincing them she could play the trumpet. She would march with the band, the trumpet to her lips, cheeks puffed out, pretending to play, her eyes fixed on the hunky hoopster. From then to her death, they were inseparable, marrying young and having two children: Nancy Anne and James Hugh. Nell had her own basketball skills, having once scored ten consecutive free throws in a contest.

All Coach's players knew and respected Nell, who always traveled with Coach, sitting by his side, whether on the bus, plane, or, after his retirement, in the stands at UCLA games. They were inseparable, devoted to each other in ways that dwarfed the romantic poetry of Byron, Keats, and Shelley. We all knew that during every game, Coach gripped a silver cross in his hand while Nell clutched an identical cross in hers. It was one of their many ways of always staying connected. We also knew that the reason practices were scheduled so precisely was because he was eager to go home to her immediately afterward.

To cocky young players in the Sexual Revolution age of the 1960s, too hip and cool for old-fashioned notions of marriage and romance, their relationship seemed cute but corny, not the stuff of dreams but the stuff of cheesy Hallmark cards. A few years later, most of us came to realize how much we used their marriage as a template for what we were looking for in our own marriages. Although I struggled to find someone I could be as intimate with and devoted to as Coach was to Nell, I certainly was able to recognize when a relationship wasn't like theirs. And to keep searching.

Nell's heavy smoking habit left her weak and sickly. In 1982, a degenerative bone disease forced her to undergo a double hip replacement. She had a heart attack during surgery, then another right after surgery, causing her to lapse into a coma for ninety-three days. Her health never recovered and, though she returned to Coach's side at games and speaking engagements, she died three years later in 1985. They had been married nearly fifty-three years.

Coach was not usually a man to indulge in self-pity. But now he struggled to recover his balance, his sense of purpose. His routine of fifty-three years had been shattered, so he tried to replace it with other routines related to her memory. He wrote poems for her. On the twenty-first day of each month, the day she died, he wrote her a letter and put it on her pillow for a night, then put it in an envelope with the other letters he'd written. He arranged her nightgown on the bed next to him. He played Mills Brothers albums because they had gone to see them after their wedding ceremony.

I called his house, but he didn't answer. I called his daughter Nan, and she told me he rarely picked up the phone, especially for anyone who reminded him of Nell. She told me how concerned she was for him. He was despondent, more deeply depressed than she had ever seen him. Even his profound faith was faltering. After all, Nell had always been the more devout one. She was the one who filled their home with religious artifacts. His love of God seemed tethered to his love of her. Without one, the other seemed hollow.

After hanging up, I was shaken. I thought about driving over and just camping out on his doorstep until he let me in. But it seemed worse to intrude on his grief. And, if I was honest with myself, I felt inadequate to the task. His grief was so overwhelming. What could I do to help? What if I did or said the wrong thing? I remembered how I had retreated into myself after the Washington, D.C., murders. I had cocooned myself while I healed. Maybe Coach was doing the same thing.

My own life was in such chaos right then that I wondered if I would just bring more anxiety. Shortly before, my house had burned down, destroying everything I owned and nearly killing my girlfriend Cheryl and my son Amir. The *Los Angeles Times* called it "the biggest monetary loss in a single-family house in city history." All my family photos, my sports awards, Persian rug collection, and jazz collection were burned up. I had another house, and my parents had just moved in with me. Plus, I was still in the middle of my Lakers season and was on the road almost all the time.

I finally spoke to Coach a few months later at one of our UCLA team reunions at Andy Hill's house. Coach and I sidled off to a corner to speak privately. "I'm so sorry for your loss, Coach," I told him, knowing how hollow those words were.

"Thank you, Kareem." He smiled weakly.

I didn't say anything. I just stared, assessing his condition.

"I'm fine," he said, by now familiar to that look of grave concern from others. "Really, I'm fine."

"Nell was a wonderful woman," I said.

"Yes, she was."

I'd run out of small talk. What do you say to a man who's lost his wife, best friend, companion? Do I ignore it and start talking about my season of basketball? Do I keep prodding his raw emotions with questions about how he's getting along?

"How's your family?" he asked. "Am I going to see Amir playing at UCLA?"

Typical of Coach to ask about others in his own time of suffering.

I shrugged. "He's got his own mind already at six. Right now he's planning to be the first black man on the moon. Tomorrow he'll want to be Indiana Jones raiding Incan temples."

"Just as it should be."

I struggled to think what to say next. Here was the one man, even more than my own father, with whom I could speak openly and freely. All those afternoons in his den in easy conversation. Now I was a stuttering fool.

"You know, Kareem," he began, draining the awkwardness between us, "when I was in the navy, the night before I was supposed to ship out to fight in the Pacific, I got appendicitis."

"I know," I interrupted. "Your college friend went in your place and got killed by a Japanese kamikaze pilot who crashed his plane into the ship." I felt embarrassed for interrupting. Why was I acting so nervous and fidgety? Concern for him or guilt for myself?

"I've thought about that day a lot," he continued.

"You mean, why him and not you? God had a plan for you?"

He laughed. "No, no. You'll go crazy thinking about stuff like that. I was thinking about the pilot. The Japanese gentleman so committed to his cause that he was willing to sacrifice his own life. One can't help but admire that dedication, that sense of purpose."

"Uh huh," I articulated profoundly. Where was he going with this?

"With Nell, I always had that sense of purpose. I knew what I was here for. To be her husband. When she died, that sense of purpose died with her."

"Coach, I..." The words came out scratchy.

He waved me off. "Have you ever known me to tell a story without having a point to make?"

I laughed. "Yes, actually. Many times."

"Well, not this time. I'm trying to tell you that I've found my sense of purpose again. Well, not found it so much as remembered it." He smiled up at me, his seventy-six-year-old face beaming. "My children, of course, and now my beautiful great-granddaughter." Cori Nicholson, his first great-grandchild, was born a few months after Nell's death. Nan had told me that her birth was the single thing that had lifted him out of his despair.

"You and I have been through the wringer, Lewis," he said. "But we're still standing. That's what matters.

Still standing and helping others to stand." He looked down as if imagining his granddaughter standing for the first time.

I had gone to the reunion hoping to finally help Coach through the healing process. I didn't know if I had, if I'd said or done anything to make a difference, to lighten his grief. But I had left feeling lighter, happier, realizing on the drive home that he had somehow healed me of my guilt. He had helped me stand.

* * *

After that night, I made sure to call him and visit him more often. Whether it was for his sake or my own, I can't be sure. I just know we both seemed to benefit from it. Most of the meals we shared were at VIP's café in Tarzana, about a mile from Coach's home in Encino. He ate breakfast there every day, even when he was in mourning for Nell. He always ordered the number two special for breakfast. VIP's owners, Lucy Ma and her husband, Paul, would sometimes stop by the table to make sure everything was to Coach's satisfaction. It always was.

He was particularly delighted this morning because the forty-five-second shot clock had finally been instituted by the NCAA during the 1985–86 season after years of Coach's campaigning. The season was over, and the shot clock had proven a big success as far as he was concerned.

"You know, I actually had my players stall back in '71 against Villanova," he said. "I wanted to prove how silly it was to allow players to stall. Must have worked, because here we are fifteen years later and they're using the shot clock." He laughed at his own joke.

"You don't actually think I believe you stalled to make a point, do you, Coach? You never did anything unless it helped you win."

He grinned slyly as he shoveled egg into his mouth. "You know me too well, Kareem."

"I'm not sure that will ever be true, Coach," I said.

"We'll see," he said. "It'll give us something to look forward to."

He was right, of course. I did look forward to our diner meals, phone calls, den lounging. Each time I left feeling I knew him a little bit better, but also knowing that there was a whole lot more left to know. It was like reading a riveting novel, knowing that there are more volumes to come. The never-ending story that was our friendship.

Mostly, it was about the continuity. The thing I had always loved about basketball was the continuity of the daily life. Not just the routine, which consisted of practice, shower, eat, but seeing the same people in the same setting, sharing those experiences with others. You'd arrive at the gym and spend hours with people who had your same experiences, frustrations, hopes.

No matter what else happened in your life, there they were tomorrow. Seeing Coach was like that for me.

* * *

When my mother started getting sick, I could feel myself withdrawing again. On the outside I was calm and decisive, the public face that was expected of me. But inside, my world felt shaky and slippery, hard to get a foothold on.

I was in Indianapolis with my son Kareem attending the NCAA tournament when I received a phone call that my mother had been taken to the hospital. Kareem and I immediately started booking a flight home, when I got another phone call telling me she was okay, but they were keeping her in the hospital for the night as a precaution. By the time we landed at LAX, Mom was in a coma. I tried not to panic, remembering that Nell Wooden had been in a coma for ninety-three days before coming out of it and resuming a normal life.

My fiftieth birthday party was less than a week away, and everyone around me had been planning it for months. I wanted to cancel it, but my dad and my friends all insisted I go ahead. "Your mother will be disappointed if you don't," Dad told me. "You know she'll blame herself." I agreed that she would, so I consented to going forward with the party. It was a lavish affair at a restaurant called Georgia that my friend and former teammate

Norm Nixon owned part of. All my children were there, people from throughout my life whom I hadn't seen in years were there. Ex-girlfriends even attended, including actress Pam Grier. A jazz band called the Ray Brown Trio was playing. It should have been the celebration of a lifetime, but all I could think about was my mom in the hospital, my dad sitting beside her bed.

Two weeks later, she died. They had been married fifty-three years, the same as Coach and Nell. At her funeral I tried to speak about what she meant to me, to everyone she knew, but all I could do was cry.

Coach called me to offer condolences. "Kareem, I'm so sorry. I know how much you loved her."

"I did." I deliberately spoke in short sentences because I didn't want to start blubbering.

"She was a remarkable woman. A truly lovely spirit."

"Thank you."

Silence.

"Don't doubt for a single second that she was anything but proud of the way her son turned out. And I'm not talking about basketball. I'm talking about your children and the kind of father you are."

"Thank you, Coach."

Silence.

"I hope you're not waiting for me to dredge up some life-affirming story or poem that will make it all better. Because there isn't one. You just get through it one day at a time."

Like AA, I thought bitterly. I wanted him to say something to help with the pain, but I knew there was nothing he or anyone could say. Words were useless. Friends were useless. God was useless.

"Is it wrong to wonder how God could be so cruel?"

"If it is, I spent a lot of days after Nell's death being wrong."

I let out a deep breath that felt like it had been pent up inside me like a caged criminal. I hadn't lost my faith, but I had certainly questioned it. Sorrow and guilt had wrapped around my heart like boa constrictors.

"We're not perfect, Lewis. That shouldn't even be a goal. It's unrealistic and unhealthy. Just be good to others and to yourself. That's enough for now." There was sadness in his voice that harmonized with my own sadness. Bonded by grief, I couldn't have felt closer to another person than I did at that moment. I breathed freely for the first time in days. The feeling passed quickly, and the sadness rushed back in. But at least I'd felt relief for a moment, which proved it might come back again and stay longer next time.

* * *

A year after my mom's death, I became aware of my dad's slow descent into darkness. Actually, it had started earlier, before her death, but she had hidden it from me. If he forgot something, she would laugh it off and make a joke about his age, and he'd laugh, too. But now that he was living with me I could see the signs that I hadn't noticed before. His forgetfulness, his occasional confusion. I'd show him photos of when he was a young, strapping cop, and he'd remember the day the photo was taken. Then I'd show him a photo of Mom, and he'd ask where she was. "When is she coming home?" he'd ask. "It's getting late." His memories were clearest the further he went into his past, until he'd only remember his time in high school and little else. His mind was on full retreat into a happier time. To him, I was standing on a distant shore, waving.

My housekeeper, Jean Herbert, did her best to keep an eye on him while I was in Arizona coaching on the Apache reservation, but Dad would sometimes slip out of the house, go for a walk, and get lost. Neighbors were always bringing him home.

After eighteen months of struggle, I decided to put him in an assisted living community where I could visit regularly and take him home any time I wanted. Then my coaching job in Oklahoma took me away on the road and I saw less of him, which only made his deterioration more rapid. Coach Wooden visited Dad at the facility without telling me. I called him to thank him.

"I appreciate the visit, Coach. You didn't have to."

"We had a nice chat. I told him what a pain in the you-know-what you used to be."

"Used to be?"

"I was being kind."

"What did you talk about?"

"Old guy stuff. Nothing to concern you, youngster."
I was fifty-three. Coach was ninety, nine years older
than my dad. I wondered what it was like for him to
visit a man nearly a decade younger than he was whose
mind was slipping away. Did it scare him? It scared
me. Was I looking at my inevitable genetic heritage?

I discussed the problem of my father's decline with
my aunt and cousin who lived in New York City, and
they offered to have him move into an assisted-living
facility only twenty minutes from them. It was the same
company that ran the one he was in; the buildings
even looked the same. He would have his own room,
and they could visit him two or three times a week,
even bring him home on weekends. I agreed, and we
moved Dad to Brooklyn.

Within the year, he didn't recognize me. He had
drifted too far from shore and couldn't see me standing
there waving, couldn't hear me calling his name. I
would call Coach to discuss what I was going through.
"It's like his body is here, but his mind is already
somewhere else," I said. Coach could only offer me
the comfort of his voice, because there was nothing
we could do to help my father.

My aunt died on December 2, 2005. A week later,
my dad died. I was a wreck, unable to make funeral

arrangements or call the people who needed to know. Thankfully, my manager Deborah Morales was there to handle everything. Whatever rope kept me moored had been untied, and I was adrift on a rough and merciless sea.

Coach called me right away. "How are you holding up?"

"Not great," I said. We had reached a point in our friendship where I no longer felt the need to put on a brave and manly face. I could be me, flawed and frightened and grieving.

"After Nell died, I said to myself that if I ever get to heaven, I'd ask God why it was necessary to heap so much sorrow on people."

"I hope you find some way to let me know the answer."

"Hey, you're assuming I get there before you. Don't underestimate me."

I laughed feebly. "I don't."

There was a long silence, but it wasn't awkward. It was thoughtful. Two friends comfortable enough not to need to fill the air.

"You remember the story about me not getting shipped out to the Pacific, right?"

As if it had happened to me. "Yup. The whole appendicitis thing."

"Right. But I don't think I ever told you about that time I was attending a coaches' clinic in North Carolina.

Something came up so I was forced to postpone my flight until the next day. Well, that plane I was supposed to take crashed, killing everyone aboard."

I was shocked. The onion had yet another layer I had never seen. "You were lucky."

"Yes, I was lucky. Twice I had cheated death. My point is, if I ask God why he allows so much sorrow, I guess I also have to thank Him for allowing me to live all those extra years with Nell. Maybe it all evens out."

"Not for everyone, it doesn't," I said.

"You're right. Not for everyone. I guess that's another question one of us will have to ask God."

"One of us, huh. I like your optimism."

"Yeah, well," he said slowly, "sometimes optimism is all you've got. Otherwise life is nothing more than survival of the fittest until you get old and die. There has to be more than that." He paused. "Like key lime pie."

I laughed for the first time in days.

* * *

I don't know if it's creepy or uplifting that Coach's favorite poem, Thomas Gray's "Elegy Written in a Country Churchyard," is about death. I heard him recite the poem on more than one occasion. There's a description in the poem of a "moping owl," which he once called me after I started wearing goggles to protect my eyes after a player scratched my cornea. "You look like a moping owl," he said with a chuckle. Every time he recited the poem after that, he would grin at me when he got to that line.

In the poem, the narrator is walking through a churchyard as night descends. As the day gets darker, so do the narrator's thoughts as he ruminates on death and its indignities. He wonders about the obscurity of those buried in the graveyard rather than the privileged ones interred inside the church. At the end of the poem an epitaph describes perhaps the poet himself:

Large was his bounty, and his soul sincere,
  Heav'n did a recompense as largely send:
He gave to Mis'ry all he had, a tear,
  He gain'd from Heav'n ('twas all he wish'd) a
    friend.

Coach offered his English teacher analysis: "The man came from humble beginnings, but because he was sincere, Heaven rewarded him. Even though he experienced the miseries that life brings, Heaven's reward was a friend." And he would look at his audience to make sure they understood.

Here's what I understood. Coach had many, many friends, the bounty of a life lived generously. When he recited that poem and got to those lines, he could have been speaking about any of a hundred people. But the true greatness of Coach was that whomever he recited it to, even if he recited it to a crowd, he made each person think he was speaking directly to them.

I know I did.

We had had our days of glory together. Our triumphs. Our accolades. That was easy. But we had endured so much heartache together, weathered so many sorrows, waded through so much grief, always pulling each other to safety when one of us faltered. That had been the true test of friendship, and Heaven had rewarded us both.

Chapter 7

Our Long Day's Journey into Night

"Players with fight never lose a game, they just run out of time."

—*John Wooden*

It is a melancholy irony that the best of friendships end in death. Those friends who grow closer and remain loyal to each other face the future knowing that inevitably one will reluctantly abandon the other to mourn that loss.

That was on my mind a lot in the final years of my friendship with Coach Wooden. As he moved deeper into his nineties, everyone could see that he was becoming frailer. His body had become shrink-wrapped around his bones, he often traveled in a wheelchair, he would tire easily. His mind was still sharp most of the time, but there were signs that he was struggling.

Everyone was worried about him, but Coach did not appreciate that. As he told each of us, quoting Lincoln, with an edge of annoyance, "The worst things you can do for the ones you love are the things they could and should do for themselves." The problem was, he didn't always have a realistic idea of what he could—or should—do.

Driving, for example.

During one of our breakfasts at VIP's in 2005, when he was ninety-five, he complained about the family conspiracy to keep him from driving. "My children don't want me to drive," he said.

I didn't want to make Coach feel bad by taking their side, but I didn't want Coach driving, either. I tried to thread the needle with diplomacy. "Why drive when you can sit in the back and read poetry? Think how many more poems you can memorize. Not to criticize, but you do need some new material."

He shook his head, frowning. "I'm not a child, Kareem."

Clearly, my clumsy attempt was too transparent. "Remember the Kipling poem you're always quoting?"

" 'If,' " he said.

"Yeah, 'If.' I remember some line in there that says something about trusting yourself when folks doubt you, but maybe listen to them sometimes."

He made a face as if I'd just ruined his favorite song by singing off-key. " 'If you can trust yourself when all men doubt you, / But make allowance for their doubting too.' "

"Right. That. Point is, maybe you need to make some allowances for your kids' doubting your driving."

He thought that over while he chewed his toast.

"In the end, you'd be making them happier and less stressed. Seems like something you'd want to do for them."

He chewed, swallowed, took another bite without speaking. When he did speak, he said, "Remember that television commercial we did for Reebok in '93? With Shaq, Bill Walton, uh..." He hesitated, searching for the names.

"Bill Russell, Willis Reed, Wilt Chamberlain," I quickly offered, worried that this was like my father's forgetfulness, a downward slope from which there was no coming back. "You walked into the room where we were all standing and said, 'Got a ladder for me?'"

His face brightened as if the whole memory had suddenly rushed into his vision. "The concept of the ad was inducting Shaq into the secret club of basketball greats. Remember what each of you said to him?"

I didn't.

"You each recited a line from Kipling's 'If' into Shaq's ear. Your line was, 'If you can talk with crowds and keep your virtue.' Don't you remember?"

I still didn't. He'd forgotten the names, but remembered my line in a commercial twelve years earlier. I smiled with relief. "Was I any good?"

He shrugged. "You were no Roger Murdock."

It wasn't until I'd gotten home that I realized he'd manipulated me away from our conversation about driving. He continued to drive until he was ninety-eight.

* * *

Bill Walton, who had played for Coach at UCLA right after me, from 1971 to 1974, called Coach almost every day. Other former players also kept in regular touch with him. I was glad we had a network to look after him. I knew that Doug Erickson, who was on the UCLA coaching staff, looked in on him a few times a week. Other UCLA staff also joined the Coach Wooden support system. Tony Spino, the athletics trainer who briefly had worked for the Milwaukee Bucks, became very close to Coach. There certainly was no shortage of volunteers. So many people's lives had been touched by Coach that they all wanted the chance to pay him back. I was happy that I had the opportunity to be one of them.

In 2006 our vigil almost came to an end. I was in Indianapolis for the NCAA finals walking through the RCA Dome with Bill Walton and Deborah Morales when Deborah's cell phone rang. Her face grew ashen. She thrust the phone at me and said, "Nan Wooden." Nan explained that Coach, who was ninety-five, was in the hospital, but they didn't yet know how serious his condition was. I was stunned. Eight years earlier

I had been standing in this very same building with my son Kareem when I'd received the call about my mother going into the hospital. I never saw her again alive. I couldn't let the same thing happen again. I told Nan that Bill and I would be on the next flight to Los Angeles. Nan protested, telling me to finish my obligations first and then come home. Coach was in no immediate danger. I consented.

I went to the podium to give my prepared speech. Instead I talked about Coach Wooden and all that he had taught me over the years, how I didn't appreciate just how much I was learning until I left. And then, surprising even myself, I started choking up. I struggled to fight back the tears, to forge ahead the way Coach would have wanted me to. But I couldn't. I started crying.

Afterward, Deborah looked shaken. "I've never seen you get so emotional," she said.

"You don't understand," I said to her, "this is my dad."

I was on the next flight. We went straight to the hospital.

"How is he?" I asked Nan.

"He's resting," Nan said.

"I need to see him, Nan." I tried to sound calm, not an emotional wreck like I felt inside.

"They have him sequestered, Kareem," she replied. "Immediate family only."

"I *need* to see him," I pleaded. "Please, Nan?"

She and her brother Jim exchanged looks, then they nodded.

"Okay," Jim said. "Come on back."

When I walked into his hospital room Coach was groggy, but unable to speak. He looked up at me, his eyes trying hard to focus.

I reached out and gently took his hand in mine. I felt tears streaming down my face. Coach's mouth moved as if he wanted to say something, but couldn't.

Nan started to cry softly. "I'll wait outside," she said. "Leave you two alone."

"No, don't," I told her. "I want you to hear this." I wanted her to know she was just as much my family as Coach was. And I wanted her to be able to repeat it to him in case he didn't hear me and I didn't have the chance to see him again.

I pulled up a chair and sat next to him, still clutching his hand, but conscious of not wanting to squeeze too tightly. I took a deep breath, looked him in the eyes, and spoke from my heart in a way that I had rarely done in my life. "Coach, ever since I lost my father, you're the only father I have. And I need you to know how much I love you."

He smiled weakly, but he smiled.

I returned to the hospital to visit several times as he continued to get stronger. I was relieved when he was finally released and made a promise to myself not to take his presence in my life for granted again.

* * *

We all had hoped his health scare would slow him down, but instead Coach seemed even more determined to follow Kipling's advice of filling "each minute with sixty seconds run." He continued to see the endless stream of visitors that trooped through his den just as he had for the past several decades. Michael Jackson, James Stewart, John Wayne, and Matthew McConaughey were among the celebrities who sat in that den. Not to mention dozens of sports superstars, many of whom were his former players. President Bill Clinton called him one day asking if he'd like to go out to lunch. Coach checked his schedule and found he already had an appointment with the women's basketball team from a small Midwestern college. Tony Spino was standing there, telling him, "This is the president of the United States. We can reschedule the girls' team."

Coach shook his head. "I don't change my appointments." He knew how important that visit was for those young women, and he refused to disappoint them. When Barack Obama was running for the Democratic nomination in 2008, he called Coach and asked him to endorse him in the Indiana primary. "I can't endorse you, because I haven't lived there for years," Coach replied. "But if I can, I will vote for you!" He did.

Despite the long list of politicians who courted him, Coach and I rarely discussed politics. He told me only that he was a registered Democrat but that he had voted for some Republican presidential candidates, including Nixon and Reagan. He was well aware that I was a liberal activist who publicly endorsed the rights of people of color, women, the LGBT community, Muslims, and immigrants. My passion for politics and desire to change the social injustices around me far outweighed his casual interest in politics. I already knew from Bill Walton, who was also an outspoken political activist, that he and Coach had butted heads over politics in the past. I didn't want that tension between us, especially at his age, so we just avoided politics altogether.

Coach traveled around the country giving lectures on basketball, teaching his Pyramid of Success, coaching young children. He wrote books, went to every UCLA home game, did extensive charity work. He even worked with grandson-in-law Craig Impelman, a former UCLA assistant coach, with his Pyramid of Success camps for kids. His granddaughter, Craig's wife, Christy, finally convinced coach to stop doing the camps when he turned ninety-eight.

That same year, 2008, Coach gave us all another fright. Tony Spino dropped by for a visit and found the ninety-eight-year-old Coach on the floor with a broken wrist and collarbone from a fall that had happened at ten p.m. the night before. Coach had been sprawled on the floor all night. When Tony asked him what he'd been doing during all that time, Coach said, "Sometimes I'm crying. Sometimes I'm laughing." When I heard about that, I made a point of checking in on him more frequently.

It was clear that he was much more fragile than we wanted to believe. I had already started to prepare myself for his death, but it was mostly an intellectual exercise. Emotionally, I couldn't let myself actually believe he would be gone from my life.

* * *

After that, things just kept getting worse.

In 2009 the *Sporting News* announced the top fifty coaches in the history of American sports, placing Coach Wooden as number one, followed by Vince Lombardi, Bear Bryant, and Phil Jackson. The magazine honored him with a luncheon in the John Wooden Room at one of his favorite restaurants. UCLA coach Ben Howland, UCLA athletic director Dan Guerrero, Marques Johnson, Andy Hill, and I sat at a table with Coach. Other former players—Jamaal Wilkes, Ken Heitz, Mike Warren, Lucius Allen, and Gary Cunningham—also attended. The running joke that day was how many of his players' heads accidentally hit the low-hanging chandelier.

Coach was ninety-eight, and that day he seemed every day of it. When he addressed the gathering, his voice was weak, and people leaned forward to hear him. At one point, he paused an uncomfortably long time. I could see on his face that he had lost his train of thought and was desperately searching through his mind to find it. Finally, he acknowledged the lapse, saying, "You get older, your memory gets a little bad, but a lot of other things get worse." This was not the first time he'd had difficulties in public. A few months before, I had seen him at the podium giving a talk about the Pyramid of Success. He never read from a prepared speech, but preferred to speak from his heart using his vast memory of poetry and literature to illustrate his points. That day he started to recite a poem, faltered, began again, then took excruciatingly long pauses between some lines. Rather than be inspired, the audience had tears of sympathy in their eyes. When he was done, they gave him one of the most enthusiastic standing ovations I'd ever seen. Afterward, he and I discussed what had happened. Coach knew he sometimes struggled and was no longer embarrassed by it. I asked him what he thought about the audience's reaction. Coach shrugged and said,

"Inspiring compassion is just as important as inspiring success."

I kept that in mind at the luncheon as I watched his former players get up one by one to offer praise for our coach and friend. When it was my turn, I spoke about how influential Coach had been on my life, how he had guided my choices, helping me mature as a player and a man. But Ben Howland said what we all felt: "He was the greatest teacher ever. His integrity, the way he lives his life, is a model for all of us."

When it came time to accept his award, Coach said with typical modesty, "No one can really honestly be the very best coach, no one." He made a nice acceptance speech, but then he paused and just looked around, slowly taking in all of these people who had come to honor him, everyone in that room was someone he loved and who loved him in return. What could he possibly say to us that we hadn't heard sometime before? "Guys," he said, "I made a mistake."

I felt my stomach tighten. Was his mind drifting again? Had he forgotten what he meant to say?

"I made a mistake with the Pyramid of Success," he said. "I left the word *love* out. And love is the most powerful word in our language and our culture." Then he went a little further. "I also want to apologize to each and every one of you."

I heard Coach speak hundreds of times over the years, and this was not his usual approach. But I could tell from the steady way he looked out at all of us, like we were all his children at a Thanksgiving dinner and he was showing us all the proper way to give thanks. I knew that he was saying exactly what he meant to say.

Looking around, I saw great professional athletes, I saw doctors and lawyers, teachers and coaches and successful businessmen. It was a room full of accomplished people. But I tried to see what Coach was seeing, and it struck me that what he was seeing was a room full of people who were successful not because of what we had achieved, but rather because almost everyone in that room had become a happy, fulfilled human being, who had taken the lessons he taught us and integrated them into our lives.

There was a lot of love in that room. Not just for him, for each other, too. We knew we had been privileged to share a great gift. John Wooden had made a difference in the life of every person there. We were all of us better people than we otherwise might have been because of him. So what in the world could he be apologizing for?

He looked out at us with love, pride, and a touch of regret. "I am truly sorry," he said, "that I haven't been able to do more to help you."

I could hear the stifled sniffling all around me. No one wanted to interrupt what many feared would be his final speech with their own tears. We all fought to keep it together until he was done.

When he concluded, all bets were off. We leaped to our feet, applauding as loudly as we could to drown out our own sobs. Afterward, we all fussed over him, kissed him, hugged him. Then we hugged each other. For that brief shining moment, we were all the loving family he had imagined us to be.

But the whole affair had taken its toll on Coach. Following the luncheon, he did an interview for ESPN, in which he had trouble finding his words. He seemed confused and embarrassed. After that day, Nan refused any more public appearances. She was determined to protect his image.

In the last months, his daily routine was very simple: watch the news, maybe some sports, take a nap in the den, read, bed. I asked him if he was in much pain, but he said that despite his many health problems, pain wasn't one of them. I chose to believe him.

Coach wasn't just an avid quoter of poetry, he also wrote his own. He often wrote poems to commemorate a family occasion: the birth of a child, an engagement or marriage. He didn't consider himself in a class with his favorite masters, just an avid amateur. To him it was a way to show his love to his family. "Good words in good order is good enough for me," he used to say about his poems. During the last few years of his life, he began collecting his poems into a book he intended to leave for his family. He wanted to include a hundred poems he had written on the subjects of faith, family, patriotism, nature, and fun. Among them is a poem he titled "On Friendship":

> At times when I am feeling low, I hear from a
>   friend and then,
> My worries start to go away, and I am on the
>   mend.
> No matter what the doctors say, and their studies
>   never end,
> The best cure of all, when spirits fall, is a kind
>   word from a friend.

In those last faltering years, his family, his former players, me—we all tried to be that cure.

* * *

In those final months, Coach had become philosophical about death. He spoke about it as if it were nothing more than an inconvenient appointment he had to rotate his tires. A nuisance more than something to be feared.

"I'm not afraid to die," he said one afternoon in his den. I certainly hadn't brought up the subject.

"Oh?" I said, uncomfortably. Not what I wanted to be discussing.

We were watching college basketball. I stared at the screen, hoping this line of conversation was over.

"They asked me the other day about my memorial at UCLA. What I wanted."

"Oh?" I repeated. I felt like a child whose parents want to read their will to him. *Too soon! Too soon!* I wanted to shout.

"The truth is, I don't think I've ever recovered from Nellie's death. Not really. So, I'm not afraid to die because I'll be with her again."

"I know you will, Coach," I said.

"Mark Twain said, 'The fear of death follows from the fear of life. A man who lives fully is prepared to die at any time.'" He paused. "Did I say that right?" he said aloud, but clearly to himself. Then he nodded in satisfaction that he had gotten it right. "I can't think of anyone who's had a fuller life than I."

"Me neither."

He looked over at me and smiled. "Of course, you still have plenty of time to beat me."

"It's not a contest, Coach."

He didn't say anything. He turned back to watch the game as if we'd never had the conversation. Maybe in his mind we hadn't. It had already drifted away with the other flotsam of forgotten memories. But in my mind, I'd never forget it. I couldn't help but wonder if, when I am near the end of my life, I'll be able to say with his same satisfaction that no one had a fuller life than I.

* * *

I will always remember the precise moment when I accepted the fact that he was dying. Sure, we'd talked about death as casually as if it were a summer cruise he was planning, and I had seen the disturbing signs of his physical decline. But there was something about his positive attitude, his optimistic quotes, his lack of complaining, that made me want to believe he could beat this particular game clock.

It was about two weeks before he went into the hospital for the final time. Doug Erickson, Coach Wooden, and I were at an event honoring Negro League baseball players, umpires, and executives. While I knew the history of those black leagues from my reading, Coach had actually played basketball against some of them when they also had played professional basketball. Though the stories he told that night I'd heard before, they were no less enthralling this time. He always spoke with such respect and admiration for the players that every black person in the room couldn't help but feel pride for those athletes who had paved the way for the rest of us.

There was so much activity that night that Coach and I hadn't had much of an opportunity to talk. I had spent three hours sitting next to Willie Mays, which was exciting for me, and had been completely engrossed in our conversation while helping him hand out autographed baseballs. As I got ready to leave, someone came over and told me Coach Wooden wanted to say goodbye. I assumed that meant he wanted to have a few parting words at the end of the event: our usual quick catch-up and good night.

I was wrong. He was in his wheelchair, looking exhausted. The event had drained him. We moved off to the side of the room by ourselves. "I just want to have a talk with you," he said. And suddenly I understood he was saying goodbye. This was the last time I was ever going to see him. I just knew it. On some level, I suspect, he knew it, too. All my emotions swelled, and I took a deep, deep breath to maintain my composure.

"How are the children, Kareem?" he asked.

I leaned forward to hear him better. "Good. Amir's working long nights at the hospital."

"It's nice to have a doctor in the family. Save you on insurance."

I told him about my other children, all moving ahead on paths of their own choosing. I tried not to sound too proud, but it was clear in my voice.

"What about you? What have you been up to?" He already knew most of my activities from our previous talks. It seemed like he just wanted to keep the conversation going, to make this moment between us last as long as possible. So did I.

I told him again about my writing projects, the books, the movies, the articles, how much joy I got from expressing myself on paper.

"The difference between lightning and a lightning bug," he said. He didn't even have to give the whole quote anymore.

"I think about that every time I sit down to write," I told him, which was true. Sometimes when I was at the computer agonizing over a word choice, I'd hear Coach's voice saying, "Lewis, is this lightning or a lightning bug?"

Then I could see by the way he sagged in his chair that he was too tired to continue. As we often did, we took a picture together. We promised to speak soon. But as I walked away, tears welling in my eyes, I had the sinking feeling that we wouldn't.

* * *

Coach was admitted to the hospital several times during the following few months. His family had taped a do-not-resuscitate order to the refrigerator. His health declined to the point that it was difficult to understand what he was saying and he didn't always seem to recognize his visitors. Finally, on May 26, 2010, Coach returned to the Ronald Reagan UCLA Medical Center suffering from dehydration.

I was in Europe when I was told he had gone into the hospital and was not expected to live. He was ninety-nine years old, only a few months from turning a hundred. I immediately flew home and drove directly to the hospital. I was very familiar with the hospital, since former UCLA captain and eventual head coach Walt Hazzard had died there of cancer the week before. And my son Amir had done a special rotation in its trauma department as part of his training as a surgeon. As I walked quickly through the maze of hallways, I felt the mixed emotions of pride that my son had excelled in these very buildings and sorrow that my last parent was dying. Coach would have said, "Balance, Lewis, balance." But I felt anything but balance right then.

Coach was sedated but still alive when I walked into his room on June 4, 2010. I felt so fortunate to have made it back in time. For me. I needed this a lot more than he did. Nan was there. She forced herself to smile, but no discussion of his medical condition was necessary. I knew; we all knew. I'm not sure if Coach was even aware I was there. I put my hand on top of his, leaned over him for a small amount of privacy, and said, "Thank you, thank you for everything you've given me." Then I whispered a Muslim prayer: "Truly we belong to Allah. Truly we will return to Him. Peace and blessings."

After that, I sat in the shadows for an hour. Doctors and nurses came into the room, fulfilled their purpose, then left. What does one think about when sitting in a hospital room waiting for your surrogate father to die? I replayed our last few visits in my mind, carefully sifting through each exchange of words to make sure he knew how I felt about him. I berated myself for not being with him more often, for not being more of the man he might have wanted me to be. But then I looked over at him lying there and felt calmness. I had become the man he'd wanted me to be. I had followed my path, which is all he'd ever encouraged me to do. I had raised my children to be kind and compassionate. I had fought for justice whenever I saw injustice. I had lived one of his golden rules: "Be more concerned with your character than your reputation, because your character is what you really are, while your reputation is merely what others think you are."

At three thirty in the afternoon I stood, said my goodbyes to his family, then left.

A crowd of students had gathered outside the hospital. Not one of them looked old enough to have been born while he was coaching, and yet there they were, holding their vigil.

I was at home listening to the six o'clock news when it was announced that legendary UCLA Coach John Wooden had died. When informed of his death, the hundreds of students outside the hospital honored him with a UCLA Bruin eight-clap and a moment of silence.

He had died with few regrets. Other than those things he had not gotten to do with Nellie, his only dream that he did not get to fulfill, he said, was to get in his car by himself and drive around the country, seeing all the wonderful things there are to see. It says quite a bit about his never-ending curiosity and the way he lived his life to point out that he lived almost a hundred years—and still ran out of time.

My phone started ringing as soon as the news was announced. "He was a great teacher and he was a molder of talent," I told a reporter. "Basketball was just the means that he affected us and made us deal with our character issues. Because what we learned on the court really did translate to our lives." The following Sunday I went to the second game of the NBA Finals at Staples Center, and when asked by a reporter how I felt being there, I said, "You should try to get through life by maintaining a balance."

Blah, blah, blah. I was mouthing Coach's words, spouting his philosophy, channeling his persona. That's what people wanted to hear. Public praise, private grief. They didn't want to hear how gray my world felt, how numb my heart felt, how I wept at home. They wanted upbeat inspiration. They wanted what Coach would have given them. I tried to oblige. Print the legend.

Several of his former players were asked to speak at a memorial service held three weeks after his death. Time had lessened the pain, but not the sense of loss. Preparing for that was one of the more difficult things I've done in my life. I wanted to keep it brief and focus only on him, but it was difficult to speak about him without referencing the influence he had on my life.

About 4,000 people gathered inside Pauley Pavilion for the service, among them the mayor of Martinsville, Indiana, where Coach had been a high school basketball star. Sitting there, waiting to say my few words, it was impossible not to look around and remember how many important moments of my life, and his life, had taken place in that building. The first time I had been there the floor hadn't been put down yet, and now a sea of championship flags hung from the rafters. Coach's teams had been a remarkable 149–2 in that building. He had coached seventeen All-Americans and twenty-four future NBA players there. That was quite a home team advantage, and this had been our home.

Several other people spoke before me. Lynn Shackelford described what we all were feeling, explaining, "We had this guide that you could always talk to...for the last forty-five years. I emailed Mike Warren and said, 'I feel so strange and odd' and he says, 'Yeah, me too.' Mike's words were: 'I felt like I was a little guy out in the ocean. I was very calm and all of a sudden it's very rough and rocky.'

"Then I thought what Coach would say. 'Oh, come on, nonsense, Shack. This happens every day. It's no big deal. You can handle it, you know what to do. Goodness gracious sakes alive, move forward.'"

None of us had discussed what we intended to say beforehand, but, remarkably, we all spoke about the lessons we had learned from him rather than the games we had won. Every one of us. A person listening to our speeches without knowing whom we were honoring would have understood he was a master teacher, and then might have been surprised to learn that he also coached basketball. When it was my turn to speak, I cleared my throat and said, "Coach's values are from another era. They were developed in an America that has passed on. I think that's one of the reasons so many people are motivated by Coach's teachings. His connections to the moral nature of his faith and his ability to convey them to us have given us the answers we need to hear in times like this. His successes as a teacher, coach, mentor, and parent are testimonies to the wisdom of how he lived his life."

We all went home that day knowing we had lost the gentle lion in all of our lives.

While that wisdom has continued to live on through the proliferation of the pyramid, his books, and the Wooden course, every once in a while there has been another kind of reminder. Less than a year after this service, Pauley Pavilion was closed for a complete renovation. In the last basketball game played before the place was closed, unranked UCLA easily defeated the then number ten ranked Arizona Wildcats. Among the players on the Bruins bench was Coach's great-grandson, Tyler Trapani. In his three years on the team, Tyler had rarely played and had never scored a point. But with the game long decided, UCLA coach Ben Howland put in his reserves. With only a few seconds left on the clock, a UCLA player took a three-point attempt. His shot was way off target and landed unexpectedly in Tyler's hands. He immediately went up with the ball. The ball quietly slipped through the net, but the crowd was not so quiet. They stomped their approval that the last points scored before the arena was shut down for renovations came from a Wooden.

Coach Howland, who had become a good friend to Coach Wooden in those later years, couldn't help crying in the locker room, explaining, "I pray a lot... To have Trapani make that last shot means so much to me, you have no idea. You couldn't have written it any better."

* * *

Some lives defy description because the people who knew that person all have different, even conflicting, perspectives. It's like the parable of the five blind men each feeling a different part of an elephant who are asked to describe what an elephant looks like. "Like a snake," says the blind man stroking the trunk. "A pot," says the one feeling the head. "A plow," says the one touching the tusk. And so on. What's remarkable about Coach Wooden is how consistent the description of him is from everyone who knew him. History will remember John Wooden for his unprecedented sports accomplishments. But his family, friends, and former players will remember him for living the teaching he most cherished: "Happiness begins where selfishness ends."

Whenever he spoke to youth groups, Coach used to hand out laminated cards that had printed on them John Wooden's Sportsmanship Pledge. Then he would ask them to make this pledge with him:

I will be a good sport whether I win or I lose.
No whining, complaining, or making excuses.

I'll always keep trying, One hundred percent
To give my best effort in every event.
This sportsmanship pledge will bring out my
    best.
Coach Wooden has taught me to be a Success.

That truly embodied the essence of what he taught about sports. Ask any player who ever learned how to properly put on socks from Coach and they will nod at that pledge and say, "Yup, that's him all right."

But for me, there was something else that most defined Coach Wooden. Not the words that he taught others, but the words that he used to guide himself. It's a poem written anonymously that Coach loved so much that Gatorade shot a TV ad featuring Coach reciting the poem directly into the camera. Anyone who wants to know what Coach Wooden thought about whenever he stood in front of his players, his family, his friends, it is simply this:

A Little Fellow Follows Me
A careful man I must be;
A little fellow follows me.
I know I dare not go astray;
For fear he'll go the self-same way.
He thinks that I am good and fine;
Believes in every word of mine.
The base in me he must not see;

This little chap who follows me.
I must be careful as I go;
Through summer sun and winter snow.
Because I am building, for the years to be;
This little chap who follows me.

I will always be proud to say that I was one of those little fellows. All seven feet two inches of me.

Acknowledgments

It took Coach Wooden and me almost fifty years to make the memories that are chronicled in this book. But it took a team of dedicated people to capture those memories and make them available to the public. Deepest thanks to Nan Wooden for all of her help and her countless efforts helping me gather my memories. To my editor, Gretchen Young, for her honesty and unwavering support to keep this book as personal as possible, and to Gretchen's assistant, Katherine Stopa, for all her help on this project. To my literary agent, Frank Weimann, for all he did to make this book a reality. To my manager, Deborah Morales, for her vision and guidance. After all, she took the photograph that inspired this book. To Raymond Obstfeld for his editing expertise, which has been essential to my success as a writer. Thanks also to all the photographers who contributed the never-before-seen photos of my life: Norm Levin, Roland Scherman, Don Liebig, Neil Leifer, David Kennerly, and Bill Ray.

Index

Abdul-Jabbar, Habiba, 230–231
Abdul-Jabbar, Kareem
    Catholic upbringing,
        170–171
    Coach Donahue and,
        122–124, 126–127
    divorce of, 233
    draft pick of, 49
    drug experimentation, 97
    education of, 31–32
    father's death, 244–248
    fiftieth birthday, 242–243
    on giving more than 100%,
        110–111
    handling grief, 232–233
    height, downside of, 77–79
    high school career, 52–55
    jazz, passion for, 65–66
    with the Lakers, 209–211
    love of baseball, 52
    mother's death, 242–243
    as Oklahoma Storm head
        coach, 222
    seeking coaching position,
        218–220
    siblings of, 35
    training Andrew Bynum,
        222–223
    on Wooden legacy, 206–209
    writing career of, 146
Abdul-Jabbar, Kareem, Islam
    and
    adopting new name, 172–173
    intensity of faith, 216–217
    religious conversion, 171–174
    talking to team about
        religion, 175–180
Abdul-Jabbar, Kareem, social
    perspectives of
    confronting racism, 128–132
    evolution as social activist,
        138–144
    filming documentary film,
        144–145
    at Negro League baseball
        players event, 268

Abdul-Jabbar, Kareem, social
    perspectives of (*cont.*)
  Olympics and, 142
  speaking at Cleveland
    Summit, 160–162
Abdul-Jabbar, Kareem, UCLA
    and
  cash poor, 80–81
  college recruitment, 55–56
  dunk shot, 104–105
  freshman year, 76–80
  interest in attending UCLA,
    59–61
  learning George Mikan drill,
    103
  recruiting trip, 20–24
Abdul-Jabbar, Kareem, Wooden
    and
  coaching advice, 221–222
  first meeting, 20–21
  lasting impressions of
    Wooden advice, 205–206
  public praise, private grief over
    Wooden's death, 273–274
  saying goodbye, 269–270
  stages of friendship, 190–192
  Thanksgiving dinner, 182–184
Adidas, 197–198
Alchesay High School, 221
Alcindor, Cora Lillian, 27–32,
    242–244
Alcindor, Ferdinand Lewis, Sr.,
    27–30, 32–33, 244–248
Ali, Muhammad, 157–160

Allen, George, 110–111
Allen, Lucius, 74, 77, 198–199,
    211, 262
American Basketball
    Association (ABA), 49
autographing sessions, 13–18

basketball, as form of jazz,
    71–72, 102
basketball skills/strategies
  box-and-one strategy, 197
  diamond-and-one defense,
    88, 197
  dunking the ball, 104–109
  flat hook, 102–104
  offensive system, 96
  rebounding, 96
  showboating, 100
  skyhook, 102–104, 106–109
Black Economic Union (BEU),
    161
Black Muslims, 230
black people in history,
    ignored in Catholic school
    curriculum, 170–171
Black Power salute, 142
Black Profiles in Courage
    (Abdul-Jabbar), 146
Bloody Sunday, 21–22, 117
Boys High School (Brooklyn), 53
Bradley, Tom, 211
Brothers in Arms (Abdul-
    Jabbar), 146
Brown, Dale, 132, 144

Brown, Jim, 160–161, 162
Buffalo Soldiers, 221
Bunche, Ralph, 60
Bush, George W., 5
Bynum, Andrew, 222–223

Calloway, Cab, 68
Carlos, John, 142
Carnesecca, Lou, 58
Catholic school curriculum,
    170–171
Chamberlain, Wilt, 54, 93, 138
civil rights movement, 21–22,
    35–38, 139, 156. *See also*
    racism
Clapton, Eric, 228
Clark, John, 221
Cleveland Summit, 160–162
Clinton, Bill, 259
coach-player relationships,
    190–191
conditioning regimen, 92–94
Converse, 197–198
Costello, Larry, 94
Cronkite, Walter, 36
Cunningham, Gary, 81–82, 262

DeMatha High School, 55
Donahue, Jack
    attitude about racism, 121–127
    coaching Abdul-Jabbar,
        53–54, 118–120
    as Holy Cross College head
        coach, 56–57

Douglas, Lloyd C., *The Robe*,
    9–10

Ecker, John, 177
"Elegy Written in a Country
    Churchyard" (Gray),
    248–249
endurance regimen, 92–94
Erickson, Steve, 256, 268

Farmer, Larry, 101–102
Federal Bureau of Investigation
    (FBI), intimidation against
    black leaders, 140–141
"For want of a nail" (Franklin), 75
Fort Apache reservation, 221
Fowler, James Bonard, 116
Franklin, Benjamin, 75
Freedom Riders, 36
friendship
    grief as challenge to, 227
    stages of, 190–192
Friendship Farm basketball
    camp, 121

"The Game of the Century," 55,
    87–88, 198
Garagiola, Joe, 141
Garvey, Marcus, 35
Gilbert, Sam, 49
Gilligan, Thomas, 21
Golden Rule of Basketball, 91–92
goodness of people, 138, 232
Goodrich, Gail, 211

Gray, Thomas, 248
Green, Johnny, 101
Grier, Pam, 243
Guerrero, Dan, 261

"Harlem" (Hughes), 147–148
Harlem Renaissance, 144–147
Harlem Youth Action Project, 37
Hayes, Elvin, 88–89
Haynes, Marcus, 53
Heitz, Kenny, 74, 98, 176, 180, 262
Hejduk, George, 102–103
Herbert, Jean, 245
Hill, Andy, 261
Holy Cross College, 56–57
Hope, Bob, 211
Hopkins, Farrell, 102–103
Howland, Ben, 261, 263, 276–277
Hughes, Langston, 147

"If" (Kipling), 89–90, 254–255
Impelman, Craig, 260
Indiana State Teachers College, 47, 148–150
interracial dating, 97–98
Islam, 172, 216–217. See also Abdul-Jabbar, Kareem, Islam and
Izturis, César, 193

Jackson, Jimmie Lee, 116
Jackson, Phil, 222–223
jazz

Abdul-Jabbar's love of, 65–66
basketball as form of, 71–72, 102
friendship duet, 72
John Wooden's Sportsmanship Pledge, 277–278
Johnson, Don, 25
Johnson, Marques, 213, 261
Johnson, Rafer, 60

Khaalis, Hamaas Abdul, 172, 229–230
King, Martin Luther, Jr., 22, 117, 139, 171
Ku Klux Klan, 39, 98, 117, 171

Lacey, Edgar, 198–199
Lambert, Piggy, 44
Lapchick, Loe, 57–58
Lapchick, Rich, 58–59
Lee, Bruce, 71–72, 228, 232–233
Lee, Greg, 101–102
legacy, Wooden's thoughts on, 206–208
Lew Alcindor Rule, 107
Lewis, John, 21–22, 117
A Little Fellow Follows Me (poem), 278–279

Madison Square Garden, 54
Malcolm X, 21–22, 116–117
Marcucci, Bob, 195, 199, 204
Mays, Willie, 269
Mikan, George, 102–103

Moore, Johnny, 101
Morales, Deborah, 6, 247, 256
Muhammad, Elijah, 230
Muhammad, Herbert, 160

Na, Lucy, 240
Na, Paul, 240
Nater, Swen, 25–26
Nation of Islam, 162, 172–173
National Basketball Association
    (NBA), 49
Naulls, Willie, 59, 100–101
Negro Industrial Economic
    Union (NIEU), 161
New York City Housing
    Authority, 141
New York Renaissance, 144–147
Nicholson, Cori, 239
Nixon, Norm, 242–243
Norman, Jerry, 27, 88, 196–197
no-water philosophy, 95

Obama, Barack, 3–4, 259–260
Olympics of 1968, 142–143
"On Friendship" (poem), 266
On the Shoulders of Giants
    (Abdul-Jabbar), 146

patience (Pyramid of Success),
    218
Patterson, Steve, 176–178
Perry, Edgar, 221
philosophies, of Wooden. See
    also Pyramid of Success

about death, 266–268
focus on activity, not
    outcome, 7–8
on giving more than 100%,
    109–110
no-water philosophy, 95
preparedness through
    conditioning, 91–96,
    99–100
on recruitment, 24–27
of "winning," 83–87
Powell, James, 21
Power Memorial Academy, 53,
    118–120
Practical Modern Basketball
    (Wooden), 138
preparedness through
    conditioning, 91–96,
    99–100
Presidential Medal of Freedom,
    3–4, 44–45
Prugh, Jeff, 199
Purdue University, 43–44, 50–51
Pyramid of Success, 19, 41,
    216–218
Pyramid of Success camps, 260

racial violence, 21–22, 116–117,
    139
racism. See also civil rights
    movement
    at basketball games, 133–138
    "handling your players" and,
    138

racism. *See also* civil rights
movement (*cont.*)
Wooden confronting,
128–132, 136–137, 148–150
Ray Brown Trio, 243
Reebok commercial, 255
Religion. *See also* Abdul-Jabbar,
Kareem, Islam and
alternative faiths and belief
systems, 170
in American during 1960s,
169–170
Islam and, 172
King and, 171
Ku Klux Klan and, 171
UCLA team discussion
about, 175–180
Return of the Native (Hardy), 167
The Robe (Douglas), 9–10
Robinson, Jackie, 59–60
Rockne, Knute, 42–43
Rowe, Curtis, 199
Russell, Bill, 54, 162

Sanders, Henry Russell "Red," 86
Schofield, Terry, 201
Schomburg Center for Research
in Black Culture, 37
"separate but equal" concept, 36
Seven Point Creed, 181–182
Shackelford, Lynn, 74, 195,
274–275
Shake, Shelby, 45–46
Shapiro, Ralph, 49

shot clock, 240–241
Sinatra, Frank, 211
Smith, Tommie, 142
"snug and tug," 73–75
social justice/injustice, 4, 98–99
Spino, Tony, 256, 261
Sporting News coaches in
history luncheon, 261–265
Sportsmanship Pledge,
277–278
Sproatt, Johnny, 129
St. John's College, 57–58
Stalcup, Freddie, 163
Stokes, Carl, 160–162
Sweek, Bill, 176, 180, 201–204

Taylor, Chuck, 197–198
team unity, 195–198
teamwork, emphasis on, 100–102
"Tears in Heaven" (song), 228
Trapani, Tyler, 276
"tug and snug," 73–75

UCLA
Abdul-Jabbar's freshman year
at, 76–80
Abdul-Jabbar's interest in,
59–61
athletes treated as movie
stars, 80
basketball team discusses
religion, 175–180
cash poor at, 80–81
recruiting trip to, 20–24

Wooden accepting coaching
position at, 47–48
Wooden as head coach,
47–48, 50–51
University of Houston Cougars,
87–88
U.S. Supreme Court, 159

Vallely, John, 201
Van Dyke, Henry, 181
VIP's cafe, 240–242

Walker, Clarence, 149
Walton, Bill, 26, 98–99, 256
Warren, Mike, 98, 262, 275
Washington, D.C. murders,
229–233
What Color is My World (Abdul-
Jabbar), 146
White America, 116, 139
White House, 3–4
Whiteriver Unified School
District Number 20, 221
Wicks, Sidney, 195, 199
Wilkes, Jamaal, 262
Wizard of Westwood, 18–19
Wooden, John. *See also*
philosophies, of Wooden;
Pyramid of Success
begins coaching career, 45–46
benching Edgar Lacey, 198
on coaching politics,
223–224
death of, 6, 273–274

defending Abdul-Jabbar's
Olympics decision, 143–144
den, description of, 68–70
on driving at age 95, 254–255
on dunking the ball, 104–105
early years of, 38–39
fan confrontation, 213–215
favorite novel, 9–10
favorite poem, 248–249
friendship with Abdul-Jabbar,
stages of, 190–192
Golden Rule of Basketball,
91–92
in hospital, 256–259, 270–277
on idea of legacy, 206–209
at Indiana State Teachers
College, 47, 148–150
love of baseball, 39
memorial service for, 274–275
on Muhammad Ali, 163–164
as number one coach in
history, 261
playing basketball, 41–42
at Purdue University, 43–44
quoting Kipling, 157
quoting Lincoln, 253–254
quoting Robert Browning, 186
receiving Presidential Medal
of Freedom, 5, 44–45
recognizing innovation,
101–102
retirement of, 209–211
sixty-fifth birthday
extravaganza, 211–213

Wooden, John. *See also*
  philosophies, of Wooden;
  Pyramid of Success (*cont.*)
  at *Sporting News* coaches in
    history luncheon, 263–265
  superstitious rituals, 183–184
  support system for, 256
  on Swen Nater, 25–26
  violent tendencies of, 45–46,
    57–58
  as "Wizard of Westwood,"
    18–19
Wooden, John, family
  at dance club with Nell, 67–68
  grief over Nell's death,
    236–240
  marriage to Nell, strength of,
    234–235
  meeting future wife, 44
  relationship with Nell, 40–41
Wooden, John, social
    perspectives of
  belief in innate goodness of
    people, 138, 232
  Christianity and, 181–182,
    217
  confronting racism, 128–132,
    136–137, 148–150
  on interracial dating, 97–98
  political interests of, 260
  on responding to social
    justice, 98–99
  supporting anti-war
    activities, 165–168

Wooden, John, UCLA and
  caring for his team, 203–204
  coaching style, 73–75, 83–85
  as hands-on coach, 6–7
  as head coach, 47–48, 50–51
  loyalty to Converse, 197–198
  meeting Kareem's parents,
    27–30
  playing favorites with players,
    195–196
  pressure to win, 192–194
  relationship with assistant
    coaches, 196–197
  at semifinals in Louisville,
    200–204
Wooden, Joshua, 40–41
Wooden, Nan
  on birth of Cori Nicholson,
    239
  concern for her father, 236
  at hospital with her father,
    256–258, 271
  limits her father's public
    appearances, 265
  Thanksgiving dinner at,
    182–184
Wooden, Nell, 44, 234–236
"Words to Action" symposium,
    162

Young, Charles, 219

Zen in the Art of Archery
  (Herrigel), 71–72

About the Author

Kareem Abdul-Jabbar is the NBA's all-time leading scorer and a Basketball Hall of Fame inductee. Since retiring, he has been an actor, a basketball coach, and the author of many *New York Times* bestsellers. Abdul-Jabbar is also a columnist for many news outlets such as the *Washington Post*, the *New York Times*, *TIME* magazine, and the *Hollywood Reporter* writing on a wide range of subjects including race, politics, age, and pop culture. In 2012, he was selected as a U.S. Cultural Ambassador, and in 2016 Abdul-Jabbar was awarded the Presidential Medal of Freedom, the nation's highest civilian award, which recognizes exceptional meritorious service. He lives in Southern California.